.

HOW TO ANALYZE PEOPLE

A practical guide with different Techniques to Speed Read People. Learn how to Interpret verbal and nonverbal cues. Train yourself to read the invisible and see the real person behind the mask.

- Jake Nigram —

Legal Notice

Disclaimer Notice:

Please note the information contained within this document is for educational and entertainment purposes only. Every attempt has been made to provide accurate, up to date and reliable complete information. No warranties of any kind are expressed or implied. Readers acknowledge that the author is not engaging in the rendering of legal, financial, medical or professional advice. By reading this document, the reader agrees that under no circumstances are we responsible for any losses, direct or indirect, which are incurred as a result of the use of information contained within this document, including, but not limited to, errors, omissions, or inaccuracies.

TABLE OF CONTENTS

How to Analyze People: *A Guide to Speed Read People With Psychology. Analyze Body Language, Personality Types and Psychology of Human Behavior. Learn Mind Control and Persuasion to Influence People*

INTRODUCTION

Psychology is such a fascinating subject as it deals with the very thing humans find most interesting, ourselves. It deals with the ways in which we interact with the world around us, and the other people in it. I believe this is the reason I spent so much of my early adult life studying the academic side of the various psychological principles. I continually get asked questions regarding certain mental tendencies, especially when it comes to analyzing themselves, and of course the other people around them.

People are always astonished by the accuracy of what I'm telling them, when in reality all I am doing is simply pointing out obvious human tendencies which everyone can see. I just direct their focus back towards it. The follow up question is then almost always the same I.e. "Do you analyze everyone you meet? Are you analyzing me now?" I never miss the opportunity to pretend that I have picked up some deep and dark secret the person has been hiding away. The momentary look of panic and shock on their face is too priceless to pass up!

However the reality is, not all psychologists are assessing everyone, all of the time. Of course we do in certain situations which would benefit us most. Or within clinical settings for instance. But you wouldn't expect a driving instructor to be assessing every driver on the road. Or an architect to survey every building they walk into.

Analyzing people is no different. You do it when you are required to do it. I have to be honest though. Once you open your eyes to some of the techniques and strategies I will teach in the following chapters, you may find yourself picking up on these tendencies a lot more quickly, and without realizing you have done so.

After all, human behavior is the most predictable thing on the planet. When you know what you are looking for. I liken it to a scene in the first Jason Bourne movie, where Matt Damon is sitting in a cafe still rather confused about who he is and what he has done in the past.

However for reasons unknown to him, he can recall every car registration plate in the parking lot has sized up all of the males in the room and knows the location of every exit. Analyzing human behavior and body language is very similar. It's about effortlessly and automatically picking up on the subtle movements and gestures of others, the unconscious mannerisms they themselves are unaware of making.

Of course you need to start out with what a person is saying. The words they are choosing to use. However this is only the tip of the iceberg in the people reading game. Words can mask intention, but body language will always reveal a person's true thinking. It will shine a light on their deeper thoughts, feelings and emotions.

In reality, successfully analyzing others is about doing two things in any situation:

1. Accurately assessing contextual cues, the character/culture and situational elements which are likely to dictate the way people are behaving.

2. Spotting "in the moment" body language signals or "tells" which give away true motive and intention.

My aim for this book is to lay out these overarching contextual principles first and foremost, to give you the grounding and a framework of reference to work with. But to also give you a look into your own behavior and psychology, to provide an insight to why people behave in the ways they do. But ultimately give you the tools and practical strategies for speed reading anyone in your daily life. So get ready for your new super power.

Have a friendly read!

Chapter 1: The art of analyzing people and how to master it

When thinking about human behavior and how to read behaviors, we must think about the animal element to human existence. We are, of course, from the same stuff as the fishes, animals, and trees. We all came from the same source, which is the magnificent and wondrous mystery or our genesis as a planet.

Much of human behavior is attributable to this- our evolution. As we progressed as a species, we developed certain cultural norms for behavior. Before that, we had to develop patterns and systems of behavior to help us survive.

This means at first hunting and gathering, and then forming farming systems and other food systems. Like other animals, we have certain mating patterns and behaviors. Like other animals, **we have sleeping, eating, and protection behaviors.**

This is important to consider when one is trying to understand human behavior. It isn't enough to consider a person's conscious state when you are trying to understand their behavior. You must think about them as an animal to truly understand behavior. As animals, we have intense drives for various things – sex, food, pleasure, and self-protection. This is where all of our drives come from, and these are usually contained in the human's subconscious or unconscious.

Sigmund Freud wrote that we had three sections or parts to the psyche.

The first most accessible area is conscious. This is the most accessible but the smallest of the three parts. The second is the subconscious. This is more repressed than the conscious but more accessible than the unconscious.

The unconsciousness, or the id, is where we have all of our animal impulses, our drives to kill and eat and survive. These are not part of the prominently conscious thought processes that we go through day to day, but they are deep below the surface affecting everything else. This tells us just how observable human behavior. There are so many deep underlying factors to each of our behaviors, and it can be extremely difficult to determine the cause of a behavior.

You can make guesses to the cause of the behavior, and there are ways to do experiments that pinpoint human behavior. One of the proponents of using science to understand behavior was B.F. Skinner. Skinner was one of the most influential psychologist s of the 20th century. He was the one who developed behaviorism, the school of psychology that purports to focus on observable, measurable behavior. Behaviorism is a school of psychology that is very science-focused and emphasizes just looking at measurable data about behavior.

Behaviorism is focused on lot letting qualitative judgments get in the way of scientific analysis. It has proven to be one of the most influential schools of thought in all of science history. What these schools of thought do is make sense of the evolutionary history of humans, i.e., why we are the way that we are. The evolutionary approach is very important to consider because our evolution uncorks many mysteries of the human mind.

We are driven by self-protection, for example. We are driven so far towards self-protection that we don't even realize it; it is just an unconscious drive that controls our wishes and animalistic desires. There are many desires and dives in the human psyche that come from our animal evolution. Anxiety, for example, is a big byproduct of our evolutionary ancestor's. Our ancestor had to constantly worry about their physical survival; they had to fight off large animals and other threatening forces to their health.

They also had to weather the elements and had to cope with the bizarre and unpredictable land of the earth without knowledge of the scientific reasons why it exists the way it does. All of these factors led to the evolutionary development of humans in the area of an anxiety response.

Humans are naturally driven to try to protect themselves, and this often takes form in the anxiety response, when the fight-or-flight response is present, and the blood will start pumping faster, the breath will quicken, and a person will feel fearful or scared.

Now, fast forward to our modern times, we don' need to protect ourselves from the same kinds of concerns. The same physical protection is needed for some situations, but the situations happen much less often, and most of the time, the negative parts of our anxiety response will outweigh the benefits of what we are getting from our anxiety state. Often, it is important to remember that repression plays a huge role in our behavior. Many behaviors are repressed, causing us to keep them building up for long periods of time. This can have several outcomes. Sometimes, the person who has repressed material will never expunge it, and it will stay hidden in their subconscious forever.

Sometimes, it manifests in behaviors like addictions or other risky behavior. Almost always, it will lead to pathology of some sort, and oftentimes, this pathology is manifested in behaviors. One often forgotten aspect of understanding human behavior is understanding the context in which it occurs and is fostered. Someone's behavior in an untouched, native land will be much different from that of a person born in Europe or Iceland. That person's behavior will be different from those that live in Mexico. There is a big difference in the way that we interact and do things across cultures.

There are, of course, some similarities. Most human tribes, for example, have some type of funeral procession. Most cultures have music that they use for different functions like celebration, war, or sadness. Most cultures have a way of dealing with grief. In some cultures, it is expressed very openly, and in other cultures, grief is expected to be a thing that you ignore completely and don't discuss. However, that is a lot of cultural differences in the way that these universal things are expressed. For example, in Montana, on a rural ranch, there may be a culture of riding horses and raising livestock.

The children in this family will learn a certain way that their duties should be fulfilled and they will have expectation cast upon them about their role in life and how they should behave. This will lead them to think this is "normal", and it pretty much is, because there is no normal.

A child who is raised in the Spanish Harlem neighborhood of Manhattan will have a different experience. Their family might have different roles in the community and the culture that the child will experience and think is normal will be the one that he or she grows up in. This is important to understand when analyzing human behavior. There is no hierarchy, no "right" or "wrong" culture, just differences. The way that one person deals with grief will be different from others and the way that one person deals with anger or sorrow could vary greatly with someone else.

The trick to understanding the behaviors surrounding certain events and situations is to consider what the person thinks is normal, what they have been raised in, and take this into account as some of the reason why they act the way they do. One should also remember that people are able to come into the culture and change their behavior and adapt to the new culture. One is able to get used to the new expectations of a place and their behavior will shift. This is known in many names, but one of them is the collective unconscious.

The collective unconscious was an idea first developed by Carl Jung, and it describes a sort of hive mind that we humans all have because of our sensory inputs. We grow from a baby inside of the womb, and each and every one of us is subject to that first experience of being rejected from the mother's womb because it is no longer our place in life.

We are thrust into the world, with no sense of where we are; only that this is a new and unfamiliar place. This is one extreme example of a common human experience. It is by these common human experiences that we can relate to one another.

One is the sun. We all experience the sun moving in the sky, in one way or another. Some of us see it for longer days and shorter nights but we all have the experience of the sun. The experience of the sun then is an experience that can be drawn out of everyone when it is evoked in art, or music, or literature.

The color of the sun is something that we all experience. The night sky is something that we all experience in one way or another. Understanding human behavior has been a task for humans since the dawn of time. There has always been a self-reflexive tendency in humans. What is the self-reflexive tendency? Being self-reflexive is what you are doing by reading this book. Self-reflexivity is the act of including awareness of one's self with the awareness of the world. It is basically self-awareness. Humans have the highest level of self-awareness of any animal, and it is our defining characteristic. We are not like the dog or cat, which we know of them as a creature but lack the awareness to carry out cognitive tasks beyond the simplest of learning.

Humans understand mostly what they are capable of. Humans understand what they once were, and what they will someday be: a baby and dead, respectively. Indeed, it is our awareness of death that truly sets us apart from the animals and what gives us a sense of how important (or not important) everything really is.

It is the awareness of death and the lack of understanding around it which has spawned major, religious, started wars and developed vice in most of humanity. It is the fear of death, which gives our animalistic drives, our most heavenly drives, and also us. It was the fear of death that drove Bach to write his famous works and Manet to paint his most amazing pictures.

This is something that you will have to deal with this your search to understand human behavior. Unfortunately, it isn't something you can get around, because it will define your very viewpoint on many important issues. The question is of god and religion. Do you have a center of faith in any religion or spirituality? If you do, that's great, and you just have to understand when that might be causing bias? If you don't, then maybe think about whom you are oriented spiritually and how that will affect your analysis of other people and how that will affect your life.

For some people, spiritual matters will not affect your life. For others, it will. It will certainly affect how you understand other people, and that is why you need to address it.

If you are not able to understand why the old lady goes to church when her friends have passed away and her family is distant, just because you don't believe in God, then you will find a lot of roadblocks on your path to analyzing people and understanding people. You must develop a sense of empathy to understand people.

And, as an atheist, (for the sake of the example) if you are able to relate and engage with the old woman who goes to church every Sunday and realize that her spirituality is a source of strength and consistency for her, and you can understand that, you will find yourself a better analyst of people. Empathy is being able to be nice to people you don't know because you have experience hardness and challenges before and you know how it goes.

Empathy is not being judgmental and empathy takes a lot of self-awareness of your context and your background. If you are from New York City and you have never left your borough, and then you leave for Kansas and live on a farm, you shouldn't expect people to act like you.

You should be able to understand that they are different people with different lives and this is how they live. In order to analyze people, you should be able to respect that. Now, this is not to say that you shouldn't rail against tyranny and forces of political and social movements that support hate. You don't have to excuse the white supremacist ideals of a person in Wyoming because they live in a tiny town in Wyoming and they've never learned otherwise because that is not how you hold standards for people.

Ignorance is not an excuse for evil. This is a somewhat controversial topic right now in the news, media, and you should be careful when discussing it. However, you should know that you should not excuse bigotry because of ignorance, that's not how it works. Analyzing people takes into account their context and all the biases involved, but it does not make exceptions for intolerance or bigotry.

Taking into account context takes knowledge of the area and history of where you are located. If someone tells you they are from Begone, New York, a small town in upstate NY, and you have never been there, you shouldn't make generalizations about the person, thinking they are uncultured from being from a small town. Instead, you should ask more about where they came from and try to learn what type of place it was. Maybe the person is from a farm town, an agricultural hub, or maybe they're from a nice suburb in Upstate NY.

However, you must build your repertoire of understanding in order to understand why people are from the places they are from. If you have the resources, try to plan a trip to somewhere you've never been before. Instead of going to the tourist attractions and doing the typical travel destination stuff for that city, try just walking around a residential neighborhood and try seeing if you can see what it's like to live somewhere else for once.

Analyzing and Deciphering Behavioral Patterns

We must look to behaviorism for our most grounded, meaningful study of behavior and analyze and decipher behavioral patterns. Behaviorism requires that one only looks at what is observable.

What are observable are mostly actions. Emotions are sometimes visible through the expression of a person on their face and body, but usually, the only real observable things we have are actions.

We also have the ability to ask people about their behavior and base research on their answers to our questions. For example, you could ask someone to rate on a scale of one to ten how they are feeling today, or you could ask a thousand people what their favorite food is. Their responses provide the data for your experiment.

But mostly, behaviorism is centered on observing the behavior and gleaning data from that. For example, if you are training your cat to respond to a bell, you will count how many times the behavior is produced by ringing a bell. This is a classic framework that helps us to understand how we can observe patterns. This is by thinking about reinforcement mechanisms. These classic reinforcement mechanisms can be used in everyday life. They are good strategies to train yourselves and others to act a certain way and are also useful to analyze others' behavior.

First, you should look for a cause for the behavior. This might be obvious or it might be very mysterious. Look for ways that you might not be noticing the cause of the behavior. Body language, to a certain extent, is not something that you can teach to someone. There are some skills that you can learn, but ultimately, it is about tapping into what you already know and what is already intuitive for you.

Analyzing behavioral patterns can be done by learning new skills, but a major part of it is trusting what you already know and tapping into the perception that you already have. Behavioral patterns are sometimes hard to see in people, as you don't have much access to their lives, but you can get the gist of behavioral patterns by observing your pets.

They are sure to have incorporated some type of habit or pattern into their lives, as we are all creatures of habit. You can start to learn how humans learn and develop behaviors by observing animals.

Chapter 2: Advantages of analyzing a person in Personal and Professional life

But having a talent and knowing how to use it are two different things. You might have perfect pitch, but it still takes practice to sing like an angel; you may have an instinctive understanding of mechanics, but you still can't fix a car until you've memorized each of its parts. Analyzing other people is something that takes work and attention, but you'll be surprised at just how many benefits you'll reap. Such as:

- **Clarity** – No more confusion when dealing with people who think very differently to you – and no more confusion when they don't react as you would and you attempts to befriend, convince or explain fall flat on their face.

- **Effectiveness** – When you are able to read another person's signals, you are also able to adjust your words and behavior accordingly. This, in turn, allows you to convey your message more clearly and effectively, which will more often lead to the outcome you were hoping for.

- **Relationships** – Some of us are more naturally awkward than others and find it tough to make new friends and impress acquaintances. When you can read other people, you can tell how they feel about you, understand what makes them happy and what they enjoy and communicate with them more deeply.

- **Safety** – Not every interaction is positive. Sometimes, you will find yourself dealing with hostile human beings who either mean you harm or are angered and likely to lash out. Knowing how to look for these signs and size up a potentially dangerous person in a single instant can mean the difference between safety and danger.

- **Success** – You won't just know how to read your peers, you will also be able to glean what your superiors are thinking. You'll know what impresses your boss and what annoys him or her, you'll know how to build relationships within your workplace and you'll feel more confident when presenting your ideas.

- **Confidence** – If you are an introvert or shy, you probably dread the idea of large social gatherings and avoid networking opportunities like the plague. When you can read people, these occasions become much less daunting – indeed, you might actually find yourself enjoying those random conversations with strangers!

- Becoming an Analyst of People

Obviously, that's not the case, or there would never be a single misunderstanding. So, before we begin to develop those skills, let's first concentrate on who you, the analyst, must become. Some of these traits will come to you more naturally than others because, just like every other human being, you are unique.

To be effective, however, you will need to hone these skills to a fine point:

- First, you must be good at paying attention to details. You need to spot the little things just as quickly as you do the big ones. If you think this skill needs work, try taking a walk down a familiar road near your home. Let your eyes wander across every surface in every direction, drilling down to the littlest of details as well as drinking in the view as a whole.

  How many things did you notice that you have never spotted before? How many times were you surprised by an entire building you've never noticed, signs of decay you hadn't picked up or little features that hadn't caught your attention? The more you try this exercise, in both unfamiliar places and locations you thought you knew like the back of your hand, the more you will hone your attention to detail.

- Second, you must become an observer. That means knowing you are not here to change what you are looking at, you are only here to catalog and understand it. The only thing in this picture that you can or should try to change is your own role within it. Before you can do that, you must observe fully and deeply and gather all the information you can.

- Third, you must set aside any instinct to judge. Figuring Out the Basics: Understanding Personality Types

Psychologists have spent decades trying to boil humanity down into categories. The result has been to create broad classes of people to capture all that diversity we boast as a species. The personality types are important to an analyst, but it's also crucial to remember that no person is going to fit into a category perfectly. Just because person A is an introvert doesn't make them exactly the same as person B. Other factors will come into play, altering how that person thinks and feels sometimes dramatically.

Person A, for example, may also be highly intuitive, while person B is not. When you interact with person A, it's hard to tell that they don't feel all that comfortable with social occasions because their intuition is helping them understand how to converse with you. Person B, on the other hand, does not have that benefit and seems awkward and uncomfortable.

That single example illustrates how the convergence of different personality traits leads to an individual, utterly unique human being – but it's only one example of thousands.

A kind person who is outgoing will more likely stop in the street to help you; a kind but shy person might be more likely to send you an anonymous gift through the mail. A person who is a born leader and patient will be an entirely different kind of boss in the workplace than one who is impatient.

The list goes on and on, but the point is made: as an analyst, you're looking for as full a picture as you can gather of the person you are hoping to read, and you may not have very long to put that picture together.

That's why it's so important to understand the personality types. They can give you a basis to work with – a starting point. It can be more than enough in a fleeting, chance encounter, especially if you have learned how to overlay observations of such things as body language and context. For those people you already know well or would like to know better, you have much more time to build a full picture. Over the top of that personality matrix, you will be able to layer your ongoing knowledge of cultural differences, social differences and the experience that has shaped that person into who they are.

Chapter 3: Types of Communication

In most interpersonal interactions, the first few seconds are very vital. Your first impressions have a great impact on the success of future and further verbal communication with another person.

When you first meet a person, you create an immediate impression of them; this is based on how they behave, sound, and look, as well as anything else you may have heard about them. For example, when you meet a person and hear them speak, you create a judgment about their level of understanding and ability and their background.

When you hear a foreign accent, for example, you might decide that you require to use simpler language for communication. You might realize that you need to listen more attentively to make sure that you understand what the person is saying.

Verbal Communication

Verbal communication is a foundation of modern life for humans. It is one of the most human traits that we have, as it sets us apart from the animals. Instead of the language of animals, we have created a language that can free us, that can be represented with asymboland have many layers of meaning wrapped up in it.

Verbal communication is often present in our lives since day one; when you are born, hopefully, you are welcomed to a world of words, sounds, and other verbal communication. As we grow up, we learn more and more words and are able to express ourselves better and better. It is amazing to watch a person go through this process, from infancy to childhood and beyond, all while developing their language skills.

Through someone's language skills, they will develop an identity. Stories are the way that we function in the world. We tell stories to communicate, whether they are formal or informal. Stories are what guides us forward and what gives us meaning. As we develop skills for language and start expressing ourselves as young children, we start to try different things with our voice and with our language. Some kids may pick up some dirty words and want to say them to other kids to get a response.

Some kids may hear things that their parents say that are too mature for them to understand, but they will use those words anyway, in an effort to "try them on" for a while. If dad often says, "Well, it's time to get to work", then his son might like trying that phrase out as well. We bounce around and absorb language like a sponge, and we are constantly participating in it.

If you look at the English language, we have many delicate and detailed nuances in our language. There is a big difference between saying, "I'd like to go to the racetrack to see the horses run", and "You want to come down to the track today and win some money?" Both are saying the same thing but use completely different words.

If you listen to yourself pronounce something that you've pronounced many times before, you will find that you squeeze the word's pronunciation and that the word has shifted over time. This is part of the rich tradition of language. There are cultural differences in verbal communication in the US as well. Someone from one part of the country may not communicate anything like someone from another part of the country.

Some people talk very quickly and like to have the pace of the conversation very fast. In some parts, a slower pace prevails. Down in New Orleans, it's too hot to talk or walk fast. Here, you'll find folks lazing along the boulevards on one afternoon talking much slower than you would find someone talking in say, downtown Chicago. So, there are regional differences in communication. Among them is the dialect. There are many dialect changes throughout even one country or otherwise similar-speaking people. There are major differences in the dialect that almost transform the language. For example, in the northern states in America, children are taught to address their elders as Mr. or Mrs. (last name).

In many of the southern states, children are taught to address their elders as Mr. or Ms. (first name). This is a subtle difference, but it can be confusing to those who have not heard it before. There are also extreme differences in pronunciation in dialects as well. Someone in the northwest states might pronounce milk more like "melk", whereas, in the south, someone might pronounce fishing as more like "fishin'".

These are rich differences that lend themselves to confusion, but also to joy and creativity. Verbal communication is a fun thing, something that we get to experience, and experiencing different dialects and language is a treat.

Verbal communication is our main form of communication, and sometimes, we don't realize how limited it is. We try to pack meaning into tiny little words that have a lot more significance than we think. When we say the word love, for example, we think of all that fits into that word. Love may mean a small favor to someone on the street that you've never met.

It could also mean a fifty-year relationship that has been rock solid since day one. It could mean loving yourself, being nice to yourself, or taking care of your physical body. Love is a tiny word but it contains multitudes. People aren't always able to fully express themselves through words. In fact, some philosophers have argued that verbal communication is so limited that we could never really express ourselves fully through words.

That's why we have art and non-verbal communication. English does a good job of quantifying things and it gives us the power to have small interactions and conversations regularly, but it is limited in how much we can actually express. Language is a blunt force tool. What does this mean? There are a few meanings wrapped up in this small phrase. Upon first glance, it says that a language is only an okay tool, not the best. It states that whatever we are trying to say, we might want to consider that we are not getting our full message out. Language is limited, and what we are thinking and feeling inside our heads is not always going to come across how we think it is.

The other part of this saying is that it is, ironically, using language! So, in order to get the point across, the saying is employing the very thing that it is criticizing: the verbal communication of language. It is criticizing the medium while using it. What does this tell us? It tells us the paradox of language. What is language good for? It is good for making small communication and making ourselves heard, but it is also most effective in metaphor and simile.

Metaphor and simile are art in language. This creates a layer of language that is not just dry communication for trade or standard purposes, but actually, using language as an art form, which can actually get your point across way better with using fewer words and actually engaging the topic. Here's a practice strategy for verbal communication: Try some phrases out that you haven't used before. A language-learning app can help you to learn a new language, which can stretch your abilities for verbal communication.

Learning a new language also helps you to connect English concepts with a new perspective. You may find ways to say things that you hadn't thought of before, or you might end up speaking a whole new language which will help you speak with clarity and precision.

One thing that is almost always good advice for people looking to improve their verbal communication is being clear. Instead of hinting toward what you what, say exactly what you want.

There are some things that are in people's way as they try to do this. One might be insecurity; the person might feel that they are scared to reveal what they actually thinking about a situation or some opinion that they have. However, obstructing your point by not addressing what you are really trying to talk about will not help you, and will, in fact, hinder your progress in learning to be an individual who does well in life. Communication is essential to every point of progress in our lives, and the more you learn to be a good communicator, the more you will find success.

Being an active listener is also a very important skill in verbal communication. Before you are able to speak clearly and express your ideas, you must first be a good listener. Being an active listener comes down to several points. One is paying attention to a person, putting your undivided attention towards a problem. Paying attention means that you are not getting lost in other subjects when you are trying to discuss something, and it means giving a person the privilege of your concentration. Another is reflecting. Reflecting is when you take something that someone has said and rephrase it and say it back to him or her.

This gives you a feedback loop to establish what you are talking about and make sure that the conversation is a two-way street. The attentive, active listener will also ask a lot of questions. Questions help a person to elaborate and it helps them to open up about a topic that they are speaking about.

Non-Verbal Communication

What's going on the entire time you are talking to someone is a whole other world of communication. We're talking about non-verbal communication. Body language. This is where people's real feelings and sentiment gets discovered.

As you probably have heard, a large percentage of language and communication is comprised of non-verbal body language and expressions. Some say that non-verbal communication is our main form of communication, and that verbal language is a less important part of our communication. Body language doesn't lie. Most of us are picking up on body language all the time, we just don't realize it. There are tiny expressions made by the body that can trigger emotions and memories and thoughts. Small, even tiny motions, can suggest some feeling to someone.

For instances, if someone makes a small turn of the head to face the other way when you walk up to them, they may not want to talk to you. This might not be something that they are doing intentionally; it is just their body language telling you what they feel right at that moment without a filter.

The person may very well want to talk to you, but the body language might be coming from their shyness. It might not be coming from their shyness, however, and sometimes, the body language is the truth. Non-verbal communication is not just body language, however. Other forms of non-verbal communication could be considered fashion, art, music, and all sorts of other kinds of creative expression. When you play music, for example, you are putting feeling and emotions out into the world without words.

People of any language can understand music because it is something that we all can relate to. Music is, of course, the universal language. It is also a universal activity, not just something that people listen to, but also do. Being a participant in music doesn't have to be hard; you can just get a small hand drum and a percussion instrument and practice between friends. This is a serious suggestion for anyone who feels like strengthening his or her perception of non-verbal communication. Get a couple of instruments that you and a friend or partner or coworker can use together. This should be a leisure activity.

Invite someone to play along with you and see what you notice. You might want to start with just a steady beat to keep the time, but as you grow more comfortable, you can get into the rhythm and try new things out. You can get a lot of mileage just by creating a pulse for others to follow and supporting them in your pulse.

Or, another thing that you can do is try out a guitar or piano. This can be practiced the same way, with a friend on the drum or percussion instrument or other instruments. This practice is a little bit different for the experience of non-verbal communication, because, if you are not practicing with a partner, you are talking to yourself. Which is fine, of course, but it doesn't help you to establish the two-way street of communication, and is then more like journaling or doing your own art on the side.

Music is one of the purest forms of non-verbal communication. It is unique in that it presents communication through sound and vision, just like talking, but it does not include words, except in the form of lyrics. Lyrics are a tricky part of the aesthetic philosophy that is contained here. Lyrics are words, but not spoken word, so they can take on a radically different meaning through singing. Thus, they are not considered verbal communication in the sense that regular language is.

The music itself, however, is one of the most mysterious formsofcommunication that we have. How music can be so imbued with feeling even though the content is a delicate and strange art. Music can be practiced over and over and studied for years, but a person may still not be able to improve.

This shows how much variance there are in the various languages of music all over the world. Not only are there different languages of music, but there are different dialects as well. Music becomes an all-encompassing trench of communication and expression and something that can hold the most mundane messages and the deepest messages that come from deep in the soul. Music is contained in frequencies, which are measurements of the vibrations of the sound waves that are created. Sound is one of the most intimate connectors we have, and many people have been exposed to the idea that music can trigger deep and distant memories for people with Alzheimer's or dementia.

This is because music is so deeply connected with our experience of the world, and sound is present with each and every experience that we have. Sound, then, becomes as important as taste, sight, touch, and smell.

It is one of the primary ways we are in touch with the world, and music often has a visual component, especially when a person is watching a performance.

The audio is really the connecting component to the heart. If you go to a symphony orchestra performance, and at the end ask everybody in the audience what they experienced, they will all have different answers. Some will say that it was of great beauty, and they felt enthralled by the amazing wonder of the orchestra.

Some will say that they found the piece to be tragic and that they felt sad during parts of it. Others will say that it didn't really affect them, and they didn't much care for the performance. Someone who doesn't have an answer for you might just make something up.

This shows the depth of the ability of music to provide experiences for people and the amazing ability that music has to create feelings and thoughts in each of us. This is on-verbal communication. You could also point out that verbal communication has this disparity in perfection as well. In a verbal communication presentation, you might ask the same audience after a speech or lecture, and you'd get similarly distant responses.

Some people would be able to sum up the points accurately, while others wouldn't be able to tell you what happens. Some would give you their opinion of the speech rather than the content. There is no accounting for the verbal or non-verbal perception of content.

Chapter 4: Analyzing people using body language

There are a number of reasons as to why people choose to hide their facial expressions. For some, it is a way suppressing their emotions towards a given matter.

As much as their words portray a particular image in your brain, it is their wish that you do not get to see their actual emotions on the same subject. For example, you may be holding a conversation with a potential partner who likes you but they are afraid to let you know that – maybe because they are too shy or unwilling to be the first ones to reveal that. Because of their unwillingness to express their emotions, they could try to fake their facial expressions.

In such a case, it is up to you to discover that on your own. You have to look closely at their faces as they speak to you so as to get their actual feelings. You never know if it could be the only thing that leads you finding one true love! Knowing about these types of nonverbal communication that exists between people allows you to interpret behavior or even predict what a person is likely to do next.

These details are wildly used in psychic reading, sales, mentalist, police enforcement, and other fields of interest that involve cold reading or any skill that requires knowing a person and his behavioral tendencies. This information also gives you a lot of advantage when you need to get to know a person better or become better at persuading others!

Face

The speed of nodding the head as you speak will indicate to you whether your listener is patient, or not. Slowly nodding shows that the person is interested in what you have to say and does not mind moving along in the conversation. Nodding quickly is a sign of impatience: the person has had enough and desires that you finish speaking sooner, or that you should allow him to talk too.

Tilting the head sideways is a sign of interest in the conversation. Leaning it backward is a sign of uncertainty and suspicion. People also tend to tilt their faces or their heads in the direction of people they like or share an affinity with.

If you attend gatherings and group meetings, you can easily tell the people with power in the group reading from how often people look at them. People who are less significant are looked at less often.

Eyes

This is the reason we talk about seeing pain, love and a bunch of other emotions, through the eyes. Some people even say that they can tell when a person is lying from the eyes.

Therefore, the next time you are conversing with someone, take notice of their eye movements. See whether the person maintains eye contact, or whether he averts his gaze. Check to see if the pupils are dilated, and how frequently the person is blinking.

Here's what to know about the eye signals mentioned above:

Blinking

Although blinking is natural, you should observe to see whether the individual is blinking too few or too many times. Rapid blinking is a sign of distress or discomfort. Infrequent blinking could be a sign that the person is trying to control his or her eye movements.

A person playing poker will try to blink less frequently because he does not want to reveal the emotions he has in regard to the cards he is holding, whether excitement or disappointment.

Eye Gaze

When communicating with a person and the individual stares directly into your eyes, it means that the individual has an interest and is paying attention to what you are saying. A prolonged gaze is somewhat threatening while constantly breaking eye contact and looking away indicates that the individual is uncomfortable, distracted, and is trying to hide his or her true feelings.

Some people believe that you holding on to someone's gaze are tough when you are lying to them. It is the reason most parents would insist that you look at them in the eyes when talking to them, and to an extent, they were right. However, everyone knows this now, and a person will deliberately maintain eye contact when lying as a cover-up. However, a majority of them overcompensate and tend to hold on to the gaze for longer, to the point that it feels uncomfortable.

On average, a person will hold a gaze for 7 to 10 seconds, but longer when listening in comparison to when the person is talking. If you hold a conversation with someone and his stare makes you uncomfortable, especially if the person is staring and not blinking, it is likely that something is up, and the person may be lying to you.

Size of the pupil

The size of the pupil is one of the most subtle communication aides. Typically, the pupil size is determined by the amount of light getting into the eye. However, emotions too cause variations in the size of the pupil.

For example, you must have had the term "bedroom eyes." It is used to refer to the look someone gives someone to whom they are attracted. For this look, the pupils are dilated, and the eyelids sag a bit. This is also the look a person gives when he or she is aroused, sexually.

Arms

Widely extending your arms could be an attempt to appear larger and authoritative, but keeping your arms close to your body is often an effort to reduce the attention of others on yourself. Standing with your hands placed on hips indicates that the person is in control and ready. It is also a sign of aggression.

Clasping your hands behind your back shows that you are anxious, angry or bored. Tapping your fingers or fidgeting is a sign that you are frustrated, impatient and annoyed. Unconscious pointing using the hands also speaks volumes. A person will occasionally point to the person he or she shares an affinity with.

Supporting the head with a hand that is resting on the table indicates that the person is paying attention and is holding his head to enhance his focus. Supporting the head with the elbows are resting on the table indicate boredom.

Hands

Hand gestures are some of the most obvious body language signals. They include pointing, waving, or using your fingers to signal numeral amounts. Some gestures have a cultural origin. However, some of the most common and popular hand gestures include:

- A thumbs-up or a thumbs-down: these gestures indicate approval and disapproval, respectively

- A clenched fist is a sign of solidarity, and in some situations, could mean anger

- **The V gesture:** this is the sign you create by lifting the index and the middle finger. The V shape created indicates victory or peace in some countries. However, in the UK and Australia, this symbol turns offensive, especially if you do it with the back of your hand facing outward.

- The okay or the all right sign: This gesture is made by making the thumb and the index finger touch while extending the other three fingers. It is used to indicate that things are fine. However, in some South American cultures, this is a vulgar gesture. In some parts of Europe too, this sign is used to indicate to a person that he or she is nothing.

Leg

Crossing your legs away from the person implies discomfort and dislike for them or the conversation. Crossed legs could also mean that the person is closed off, or is looking to have some privacy.

Feet

When a person is sitting or standing, the direction to which the feet point is the direction the person wants to take. This could tell you whether the person considers you favorably or not. This cue is relevant both when having a one-on-one conversation and when talking in a group. In a group setup, the direction to which the people are pointed will tell you a lot about the group dynamics. If you are having a conversation with someone, but his or her feet are pointing in someone else's direction, this is an indication that the person would instead be talking to the person to whom his feet are pointed towards, regardless of the cues you get from the upper body.

Chapter 5: Identifying specific personality traits through body language

Realizing that areas of your personalities are engaged at different levels daily at work, home and play - is one thing, and understanding how to use that knowledge is another. But it is very vital.

When you can identify personality types, it can assist you to exert your influence, enhance relationships, communicate effectively, and accomplish success in whatever desire is in play. In this section, you will understand the different personality types and their building blocks, and you will realize that the personality type traits are what makes us all the same and at the same time it makes you different from the rest.

Ensure that at the end of the study, you figure out where you lie in the sixteen personality types. Personality type is defined as the psychological categorization of the various kinds of individuals. Personality types are sometimes separated from personality traits; the latter embodies a less categorization of behavioral tendencies. Personality types are also said to engage qualitative differences among people, while traits might be construed as quantitative differences.

Leaning

People lean forward to things that they like or feel attracted to you. It is a good sign when someone leans toward you. If someone is really listening to you or really likes you, he will lean toward you or position his torso to face you.

However, if someone leans his torso away from you that indicates that he is going through some type of stress. Either he does not like what you are saying, or he is having some sort of negative reaction to you as a person. This reaction is also not always directed toward you. You may also notice someone pulling away from you and leaning away from you if he receives bad news in a text message or phone call or sees something that distresses him.

Hands

Really watch someone's hands. What he does with his hands indicate a lot about what he is feeling. His hand movements are an even better indicator of deception than his eye contact. Fidgeting or constant hand movements indicate intense nervousness. If someone tries to make smoothing gestures with his hands, he is probably lying. If he is balling his hands into fists, that indicates aggression.

Fidgeting and Pacifying Gestures

Fidgeting is a sign of nervousness and emotional distress. Picking at one's nails, rubbing one's thighs or forehead, and scooting around in one's seat are some of the forms of fidgeting that indicate that someone is experiencing some sort of emotional duress.

This emotional duress may be related to the conversation. It may be because he is lying to you and feels guilty and nervous about getting caught. It may even be because he is going through something bad in his life and it is manifesting even though he is trying to focus on talking to you. Especially watch for pacifying gestures. This is any kind of rubbing or smoothing motion that a person performs on his own body. When someone rubs himself in any way, he is trying to soothe himself. Consider what he may be trying to soothe himself about.

If you are talking about his job and he starts rubbing his forehead while telling you that everything at work is stellar, you can assume that there are problems in his work life. If he repeatedly rubs his thighs while bragging about what a great guy he is, you can safely assume that he is thinking of all the ways that he has been a bad guy and he is trying to soothe his guilt. When you bring up a subject such as divorce, you can tell that someone is distressed by the topic by his sudden influx of pacifying gestures. A person who is constantly trying to pacify himself during a normal conversation is probably socially anxious.

If someone touches the crook of his neck, this is a gesture of discomfort and even fear. The throat is vulnerable, so when a person grabs at it or touches the crook of it, this is a self-defensive gesture. This gesture can show that a person feels threatened by you or someone else that he is talking to. Also, this gesture is most common in women rather than men. Watch for women who perform this fidgety gesture around their husbands or boyfriends as a clue about abuse.

Facial Expressions

Facial expressions essentially leak someone's internal emotions. This leakage is very hard for people to control. Most people can't control it and their initial reactions to things will flash across their faces before they regain control and put on their normal social mask of a smile or serious frown.

If you bring up a subject and you notice that someone suddenly clenches his jaw or furrows his brow, you can assume that the subject upsets him in some way.

A person who attempts to act serene or happy yet keeps clenching his jaw is probably either an aggressive person at heart or has something upsetting on his mind that he is not telling you about. Tense facial expressions in someone's baseline often indicate that someone is naturally tense and aggressive, insecure, or often depressed.

If you notice a brief smile, you can tell that something brings someone great pleasure. Watch for brief flashes of mirth when you are talking about upsetting or serious subjects. This can indicate that a person gets sadistic pleasure from the upsetting subject matter. This is a troubling sign of sociopath or psychopathy. Alternatively, if someone can't hide his mirth at a serious matter, you can assume that he doesn't take things seriously and lacks proper respect. Facial expressions tend to leave their marks on people's faces. Most people adopt a general mood based on their outlook on life. This general mood is reflected in a general facial expression.

As people wear certain expressions over time, these expressions carve permanent wrinkles or grooves into their facial tissue. People who are often depressed will have frown lines in their brow and on either side of their mouths. People who are generally jovial will have laugh lines and dimples from smiling. People who are often angry will have tense lines around their eyes and a hard gaze. Lines along the top of the nose can indicate someone who is frequently wrinkling up his nose in disgust and hence is a very critical and judgmental person.

Silence

If someone takes a long pause, clears their throat, or falls silent, then they are trying to think of what to say. They may be stalling for time as they manufacture the best response. They may just be waiting for you to offer guidelines about where the conversation should go.

Silence is not always bad. You should listen to your gut about it. If there is an uneasy vibe with the silence, then you can safely assume that the silence is not natural and easy. If there is a comfortable vibe, don't doubt that and make yourself nervous. You can enjoy silence with someone if it feels right to you.

Eye Contact

Eyes are considered windows into the soul because of the wealth of information that they provide about a person's emotional state and feelings toward you. Eye contact helps maintain emotional connection between people. Changes in eye contact can break the connection or show problems within it.

When someone closes his eyes, this is a sign that he is thinking really hard about his response and is stalling for time. This does not necessarily mean that he is thinking of a lie. But it can mean that this subject is difficult for him to talk about, either emotionally or mentally, and he needs time to think of the perfect words. A lack of eye contact can indicate that someone is not comfortable in what he is telling you. This is not necessarily a sign of deceit. It could just be a sign of nervousness or shyness. It can also be a sign that someone feels ashamed of something. A lack of eye contact is often cited as an accurate way to spot deception, but in fact good liars are perfectly able to maintain normal eye contact while lying. Eye contact is not the best gauge of deception.

Piercing eye contact can make you uncomfortable, and for good reason. Someone who looks into your eyes too piercingly is likely searching you for information. He may be trying to force a connection on false grounds. Too much eye contact is a better indicator of deception than lack of eye contact, as a matter of fact.

Pupils

Another clue that eye contact can offer is pupil dilation. If someone's pupils dilate around you that is a sign that he likes you or likes what you are saying.

During a business meeting, you may notice that your client's pupils dilate when he hears that he is about to make bank on a new product if he chooses to invest. When you are trying to sell something, pupil dilation indicates that someone is interested. Watch for pupil dilation in your dates, too, to tell if they really like you.

Pupil constriction means the opposite. When someone's pupils constrict, he isn't happy with what he sees. He is displeased and pulling away emotionally. He may be upset and bothered or seriously offended. Watch for pupil constriction in people when you bring up unpleasant subject matter or when a gruesomely violent scene occurs during a movie.

Breath

Someone's breathing rates indicates his heart rate. His heart rate indicates his emotional state. Someone who is calm will have normal, level breathing, while someone who is upset will have more rapid breathing.

Do not read too much into breath, however. Some people have health issues that affect their breathing rates. Exercise, high wind, allergies, and other factors can all make someone breathe heavily around you.

However, you cannot ignore things like heavy exhales or sharp inhales. These indicate someone's immediate emotional response to something. A sharp inhale often shows that someone is shocked or surprised. A long, heavy exhale means that someone feels defeated and is under intense emotional distress. Often a liar will make this exhale when he has been caught in a lie.

Walking

How a person walks suggests a lot about his confidence and what he is feeling. A confident person walks with big, firm gestures and keeps his spine straight and his head held up straight. You want to deal with confident people, as they know how to take care of themselves.

Less confident people will shrink into themselves. Their shoulders will be hunched, their heads will be held down, and their spines will be slouched. They will probably shuffle along, trying to avoid attracting too much attention. A person who is sad may also walk like this. A happy person will bounce along, showing his joy in big movements. An angry person will usually be tense, with his fists balled up and his shoulders forced up.

Guessing Peoples' Hidden Intentions

Context can play a huge role in accurately assessing the momentary behavior of others, and credence should certainly be given to the situational settings you find yourself in.

Discount any contextual etiquette within formal and business settings for instance. These factors shouldn't be the only lens by which you are assessing somebody's intention with regards to their body language, but considerations that would be wise to take on board nonetheless. However analyzing people isn't just about mannerisms and gestures. You do still have to pay attention to the words these people are choosing to use.

Care must be taken here as language can be a great mask for intention. However you can still deduce a great deal about a person's mindset if you know what you are looking for within their vocabulary. This will come down to the adjectives and describing words the person chooses to use. The emphasis they place on the base nouns and verbs within their sentences to accentuate meaning. This will show much about their current mindset.

Deceit

Wouldn't it be nice if you could tell when people are lying to you? Your lie detector will become much stronger if you watch for these signs in people. Once you are able to determine when people are lying, you possess a great deal of power. You can really encourage honesty and you can offer consequences to the liars in your life.

Most people do lie. The worst liars in your life are probably people that you actually know quite well. Your significant other is shown in studies to be the most likely to lie to you. From little white lies to keep the relationship healthy to big lies about where he or she was last night, you can expect your lover to lie. But family members and friends and business partners are all equally capable of lying as well.

Many people use deception as a means for survival; lying is shown to start as early as infancy. You don't have to tolerate lying, however. Demand that people respect your intelligence and treat you with integrity and honesty.

Difference from the Baseline

Marked differences in someone's behavior from his usual baseline is a good indicator that deception is going on. His gestures, body language, eye contact, and tone will differ from the usual. You will wonder why he is acting so strangely. The likely answer is that he is being less than truthful with you.

Quavering Voice

Someone who is nervous and suffering from a lot of emotional tension will have a quavering voice. It is difficult for most people to tell bold, direct lies. So when they do, they have a lot of trouble talking to you directly. They won't want to speak in a normal, confident tone because they lack confidence in what they are saying.

Sweating

Lying takes a lot of effort. The thought of getting caught is quite scary. Therefore, a liar is often under intense emotional stress while lying. He will start sweating. You will notice beads of sweat forming on his face, particularly along his brow and temples. If he frequently wipes at this sweat to hide it from you, that is an even greater affirmation that he is lying.

Grooming and Cleaning Gestures

A liar can feel dirty from his lies if he has a conscience. Therefore, he will try to placate his sense of dirtiness by performing grooming gestures. He may smooth out his tie or the wrinkles in his pants. He may pick at his nails, inspecting them for cleanliness. He may even groom his hair or facial hair.

The key to watch for is when he does these things while talking to you. His grooming habits will interest him much more than looking right at you. In addition, neatening or organizing things while talking to you also indicates deception. A liar will straighten out stacks of paper on the desk in front of him or will preoccupy himself with cleaning things while avoiding looking at you.

A lie can make someone feel disorganized, as someone attempts to straighten out his story. Therefore, his efforts to create a neat and tight story will manifest in him organizing things around him.

Mismatched Cues

His gestures and body language will not match his words. He may be saying that he is happy, but the unhappy droop in his shoulders will alert you otherwise.

He may be saying that he is not lying to you, but meanwhile he is hiding his hands from you.

Usually people are consistent between their nonverbal and verbal communication. Inconsistencies are cause for alarm. When an inconsistency exists, someone is experiencing a mismatch between what he says and what he feels. This is a good sign that he is not telling the truth. You can spot even tiny white lies this way.

Mismatched Verb Tenses

Most people tell their stories in a specific order: back story, main content, and aftermath. Most people will use the past tense, since the story occurred in the past. If at any point during the story someone switches to a different tense, namely the present tense, then you has a good indication that something is not entirely truthful in the story that he is telling. A person will switch to the present tense because his mind is busy manufacturing details in the present as he tells the story. Therefore, the present tense often indicates that a story is not truthful. Rather, it is made up on the spot.

Descriptive Vagueness

Remember how I said liars have a tough time being direct?

A liar will be very vague in his language because he has trouble being direct due to his lack of honesty. Therefore, watch for intentionally vague language and word choice. For instance, if you are accusing an employee of not locking the doors to your store last night, she may lie and say, "But I swear that the door got locked." Notice how vague that statement is. She doesn't directly say that she herself locked the door. She uses the passive term "got locked."

A liar will try to remove himself from blame or from a situation that he does not want to be implicated in. He will do this with more passive language. A person who is being honest will usually use more direct and non-passive language.

Lessening the Impact

A liar will try to lessen the impact of what he is being accused of by choosing words that carry softer connotations. Someone who is lying may choose a word like "taken" over "stolen," or "stepped out" instead of "cheated." He will pick words that make what he did seem less offensive. This is his way of trying to lessen the impact of what he did and trying to convince you that what you are upset about is not that big of a deal. He is essentially trying to take the heat off of himself. But don't fall for this.

Defensiveness

A liar will get defensive if you confront him. Instead of just saying that he is being honest, he will try to manipulate you into feeling bad for doubting his honesty. He will say things like, "Why wouldn't you believe me?" or "Would I lie to you?"

He may also act angry and ask why you have the nerve to question his integrity.

Some key terms to watch out for include:

> "Why would I lie?"
>
> "Would I ever lie to you?"
>
> "You know me. I'm not a liar. And I hate the accusation."
>
> "Have I ever lied to you?"
>
> "Why wouldn't you believe me?"
>
> "You can believe me or not. It's your choice."
>
> "I swear to God/I swear on my mother's grave."
>
> "You won't believe me, I know, but I wouldn't lie about this."

An honest person may get defensive too. But this is because he is desperate to get you to believe him. He will probably say things more like, "I am being honest," or "I am an honest person. Please believe me."

Sharp Exhale

A sharp exhale can indicate when someone has been caught. If you confront someone about something and he sharply exhales, you can assume that he is probably guilty. An exhale is an automatic reaction that many people have to getting caught in some sort of lie or other action. It is a sign of emotional distress, often guilt.

Clusters of Actions

Often, a single action does not offer very much information about someone. But clusters of actions can really tell you if someone is lying. A liar will usually have more than just one tell. Watch for several aberrations in behavior to clue you in on his honesty.

Manipulation

Have you ever met a seemingly really nice person, then find out that he or she is just using you? After a while, you start to notice that you are being manipulated. You get that yucky feeling that you don't matter to the person. Well, you can avoid that yucky feeling altogether by recognizing when someone is manipulating you.

Manipulators are typically emotionally stuck in childhood. They have never developed the proper adult skills of communication. Because of how they were raised, they found that playing games were more effective at getting them what they wanted than just asking. But they never outgrew this and adjusted to normal adulthood. Now, they feel that they must play games.

On the other hand, some manipulators are sociopaths. They have literally no empathy or compassion for others. They view other people as tools that they can use to their own ends. No matter why someone is manipulative, you do not deserve that kind of treatment. You are not a pawn for someone to use. You should learn to identify this behavior to avoid a lot of problems and hurt in the future. Remember that you can never change a manipulator. Besides, it is not your job to heal or change a manipulator.

Flattery

A manipulator will be great at making you feel like you need him in your life. He gets an emotional hook into you by first making you feel like you depend on him for your happiness. He will flatter you and charm you until you just can't get enough. However, this flattery is all fake. Somewhere in your gut you will probably feel that is fake. Whether you feel that eerie sense that something is not right or not, just be very wary of someone who is too nice.

Lots of Small Favors

Watch out for someone who is extremely generous right after meeting you. Usually a stranger is not so nice. Therefore, a lot of small favors are a bad sign. It means that someone is trying to put you in his debt. He is doing you a lot of favors to get you to feel like you must do things for him in return. He is essentially collecting favors to call on for later.

Threats

The other trick that a manipulator uses is getting you to feel too scared to do anything without him in your life. Whether he is a romantic partner or a business partner, he will use threats to make you feel like only he would want to be around you.

He will make it seem like you are a horrible person and only he is able to put up with you. He will do this so that you feel as if you cannot do anything without him. You feel that he is the only one who will tolerate you, so that you never leave the situation with him. A manipulative person will start doing this relatively quickly after meeting you. He knows that in reality he is a terrible person with little to offer you.

Therefore, he will want to ensure that you never leave him and move on to someone better for love, business, friendship, or anything else.

Drama

A manipulator will try to create a lot of drama in your life. By creating drama, his aim is to get you to relent to what he wants just to end the drama. He tries to make your life miserable until you give in.

He may also try to create drama in order to drive away your loved ones and friends. That way, he can isolate you. When you are isolated, you are vulnerable. You have no one to protect you or tell you that you are being treated wrongly. A manipulator likes to have you in this spot so that he can exploit you.

Guilt

One of the most powerful human emotions is guilt. Guilt will make you do things just to escape the feeling. Manipulators understand this fact. As a result, they love to use guilt to make you feel bad so that you do what they want. They are fantastic at making you feel guilty just for being alive.

If someone frequently makes you feel guilty or ashamed, then you are being manipulated. No one who cares about you will make you feel this way. A stranger certainly has no right to make you feel this way. Watch for people that frequently bring up your mistakes, tell you that you are a bad person, or tell you that you are somehow inadequate.

Watch for people who act put upon when you ask them to do things, so that you feel guilty just for asking. These are all signs of manipulation and you should run far away when you encounter them, especially in people that you just meet.

Behaving Unbearably

Another form of manipulation is when a person throws a childish fit rather than acting like an adult. He will sulk, pout, yell, or otherwise act like a jerk until you do what he wants. He gets his way by making you miserable. You finally do what he wants just to get him to stop.

An example of this is when you want to go to a certain restaurant to meet someone. He doesn't really want to go there. But instead of telling you that, he comes along to the restaurant and then pouts the entire time. He makes you so miserable that you finally just want to leave the restaurant.

He Won't Tell You Things to Your Face

If a manipulator is unhappy about something, he will not have the strength to tell you to your face. Instead, he will tell everyone else in the world but you. He will make sure that it gets back to you through other people how unhappy he is. In this way, he tells you how unhappy he is without having to tell you himself. He avoids confrontation in a very chicken way.

For example, someone might tell you that he is happy to work for you late. But then he complains to the entire office about how you shoved off your workload on him. You find out how unhappy he is to work for you from everyone in the office. He could have just told you no to your face.

Lying

A manipulator is usually also a liar. If you frequently catch someone lying to you, you should watch out. You do not need liars in your life. But usually a liar brings loads of other problems along with him.

Refusing to Take Blame

If someone does something bad to you, you will naturally want to confront him. But if he immediately twists what he did to you to seem like your fault, then he is manipulative. He will be adept at making you feel as if everything is your fault. He will have an amazing way of always escaping blame. Also, he will never, ever admit to wrongdoing and he will never say that he is sorry for anything.

Chapter 6: Human mind: the endless mystery

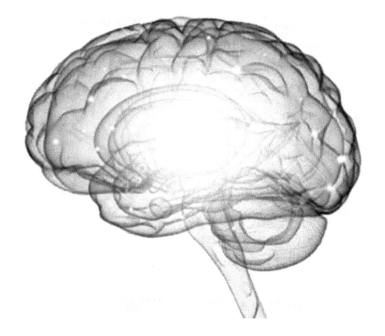

Human beings are fascinating creatures, complicated to the point of lunacy yet achingly simple at the same time. No two human beings think alike, nor have the same experience of life to base their opinions on, nor make the same decisions in the spur of the moment, yet we are all driven by the same desires: love, safety, comfort and so on. We take different paths to the same conclusion, each of us as unique as a star in the sky. So how, as an onlooker, can you possibly analyze even one human being? Should it not take days, weeks, and months to understand what makes that person tick and predict how they are likely to react?

Not necessarily. To understand human beings, you must first acknowledge that all of us are just points on a range of bell curves. Each of those bell curves represents a characteristic or trait – optimism, empathy, kindness and so on. You may be as kind as it's possible to be, you may be as cruel as it's possible to be or (more likely) you fall somewhere in between. You could be more quick to anger than anyone else, you might be the slowest to anger of anyone, or (more likely) you fall somewhere in between.

If you're not familiar with the bell curve, it's called that because it's a hump with the largest portion in the middle. At either end are the outliers – the smallest number of people will meet those standards? Most of us lie somewhere near the center of the bell curve, at the highest point, or skewed slightly to its left or right.

When you begin to understand that we are all simply a collection of characteristics, each of them interacting with one another to produce a unique personality, it suddenly becomes easier to accept that reading and analyzing a human being is possible.

So how do you do it, and why would you want to? We'll take a closer look at these questions as we begin to dive into this crucial skill. As philosophy developed in the West, we became obsessed with separating the mind and body. The indecent philosophers of greatness like Aristotle and Plato have provided the foundation for thousands of years of philosophy that sought to state that we had been prisoners of the body and that the mind was the holy part of the human.

This attitude basically makes it seem like the mind is the godly part of the human and the body is the animal type part of the human. This is a classically Christian view, as the Christian view states that man was made in God's image. If we are made in God's image but as humans, we must have some part of both, and to the ancient thinkers, the mind seemed more god-like. Of course, the body has to deal with waste and food and sights and smells that seem quite unsavory.

The mind, in contrast, deals with matters of cognitive ability and feelings and reason and science. This was the classical attitude toward the mind-body split, and it was a good thing because the mind is godly and the body isn't. What these ancient philosophers forgot, though, is that our most human part is not the brain or the mind or the hands, but actually the big toe. Not just any of our toes, but particularly the big toe.

The big toe is what separates us from the other animals physically. It is what lets us stand up, and not be all wobbly, and lets us develop incredible athletic feats like running and sports.

Mindfulness is interwoven into almost every subject discussed in this book, and it is definitely interwoven into the mind-body connection. Most of us these days grow up with a relationship far too focused on the mind. We must remain positive and working for capital gains constantly to be able to have our lives go on. We are subjected to modern media, which is all-pervasive, and this affects our cognitive structure as well. We are mostly told to ignore our bodies in order to work eight-hour shifts standing or sitting.

When you do this kind of work, you have to do extra to keep up with the demands of the body, because the body is not designed to be happy when it is inactive for most of the time. The body craves engagement and interaction in the world. The body needs to be a part of the world and to do that, it must interact with the world in a physical manner. This can be accomplished in many ways buttheeasiest is directed exercise, whether just running or walking or some other form. For most of us, the transition that needs to happen is to be more toward the body from the mind. This is because we are slanted too far in one direction. Therefore, we need to make up for this disconnection and find a way to be more oriented toward the experience of the body in different moments to take information in.

The mind/body connection is important because you can't be integrated without it. An integrated person is not only one who has experiences and knowledge but also has the ability to synthesize different ideas and concepts to build beliefs and success through behaviors. This is the difference between knowledge and wisdom. Knowledge is a knowing of some information and data. Wisdom is the ability to really know what the information means, for them and for others and the ability to employ information in different ways.

The mind-body connection is an illustration of the ultimate integration that a human could hope to achieve. By achieving high levels of awareness and mindfulness, a person can develop their personality beyond their current state of development towards self-realization. Self-realization is the concept that a person can be so integrated and truly act in their authentic self, rather than keeping it rewrapped in layers of repression and denial. It is when a person is no longer concerned with what the world thinks about them, and they act totally honestly. It is a state where you do not doubt yourself because you are confident and ready to engage with whatever comes along.

It is a state of being you. Most people are far from this, and they have things that stand in the way. One thing that stands in a lot of people's way is youth. When we are young, we don't have experiences in the world to look back on and draw information from. This makes us so confused about where to go and dealing with our problems. Self-realization, then, is something that probably comes later in life than adolescence and young adulthood. It is usually someone somewhat advanced in their years, who has do a lot of soul-searching, tried a lot of things out, and done a lot with their lives. These are people who are usually good candidates for this type of transformative experience.

Part of getting there, besides experience, however, is awareness of the body. Awareness of the body has been so demonized in our culture that we are only rewarded for what is visible in our cognitive accomplishments and we are torn desperately away from things that will keep us healthy being connected to our self and earth. The mind-body connection is extremely important because, in order to read body language, a person must have a balance between their cognitive mind and their emotional mind. The emotional mind is more focused on the unconscious, which is giving us information as to our animal selves.

This is really where the rich analytical body language stuff comes into play, but it has to be tempered by the cognitive state of mind, the thinking mind.

The thinking mind is able to take the information from the emotional mind and really interpret it into something that actually means something for us. We can't be working in either of these minds exclusively, and that's why you need to foster a balance in the mind-body connection. A person who is too much in the mind will over-process things, and a person who is too much in the emotional mind and the body will not be processing enough.

They will be taken over by the impulses of the animalistic side of our minds, and they will not be able to process body language information, but rather be overtaken by the information and too involved to have a sense of self around it. You see the first one all the time: people too much up in their heads. These are people who worry a lot and can't be in the present moment.

You may know someone like this. They might come off as whiny or complaining or too self-oriented. This is because they are a slave to their mental habits, and their mental habits just happen to be thinking negative thoughts about themselves and others.

This is fine, and they are not bad people for it, but it isn't the healthiest way to live and if you search deeper and connect with the body, you can change his fate and be a balanced individual. There are some who are too in the body and they never process in a cognitive manner that they are experiencing. This may include addicts or people who have trouble with eating or sex addiction. The addict is not concerned with the future when they are taking a drug; they are only thinking about the present.

This is obviously not good for them, but it doesn't line up with the idea of being present. Why? Because we are not doing things in the present moment with enough intentionality. Intentionality is the difference between an addict's mind and a well person's mind.

The well person is able to act with intentionality because they know that if they partake in a certain experience; they will know that it will affect their day. They have that knowledge and they use it. An addict does not have the knowledge, and when they do, they are not able to use the knowledge. An addict is not only exclusively in the body and emotional mind, however, and sometimes, they are skewed too far towards the head; they are always up in their thoughts. This is the type of addict who is good at rationalizing and hiding things.

This is the addict who is functional and smart and capable but never changes. If this type of addict chooses to get more in touch with the body and address the mind-body connection, they will start to come out of their heads and they will start to realize that we all have a common experience in our bodies.

Once the addict realizes that we all have a common experience and we are all trapped in our bodies, they start to realize that they no longer have to suffer from their condition like they used to. They can learn new ways to deal with their condition.

Chapter 7:
Clues that reveal it all

When it comes to reading people, sometimes you cannot learn a lot about a person based just on how he acts on a first meeting. Behavior can be extremely deceptive, especially during a first meeting when someone is putting on the charm for you. But watching someone's behavior over time and observing someone's past for clues about their general behavior can give you a lot of clues about a person's real personality.

Past Behavior

You should get to know a person the best that you can. That way, you can observe patterns in his general behavior. You can also hear more and more stories about his past, as well. Generally, someone will open up to you and tell you about his past. From his past behavior, you can gather a lot of clues about who he is.

A long string of bad relationships or several divorces are one warning sign that he is unable to be a sensitive and communicative lover. It is likely that he is unable to learn from his mistakes, as well. If he has a lot of enemies that suggests that he is a hard person to get along with and he may be a traitorous personality. A history of spending money frivolously, large amounts of debt, poor financial decisions, and gambling indicate poor planning and an inability to handle his life.

Someone who frequently gets into trouble with the law by fighting or other behavior has poor impulse and poor emotional control. If he frequently bails on plans and doesn't demonstrate any follow-through, then he is probably not someone to trust with any serious commitment in business or even romance and family. One thing to really watch out for is someone who has kids with many different people. This shows a huge lack of responsibility and an inability to commit.

It is true that people can change. Just because someone screwed up when he was younger does not mean that you should judge him for the rest of his life. However, repeated behavior indicates that he never learned from his mistakes. This is very troubling. Even if he says that he has learned his lessons, his repetition of the same mistakes is living proof that he has not. Watch for repeated mistakes or very recent mistakes that show that he has not really changed.

Earlier I mentioned that you should never judge someone based off of behavior only. While this holds true, repeated behavior is something that you can safely judge. A person who does the same things over and over is likely rooted in such behavior. Watch how someone frequently acts around you. Watch for patterns in behavior. Patterns should never be ignored.

Reputation

What other people say is not always reliable. You can't believe everything that you hear on the rumor mill. Sometimes, people will have a vendetta against someone and will spread vicious rumors. Sometimes, just one person is able to spread enough false information about another person to create his bad reputation.

But usually, a large number of people don't conspire against one person. If you hear several people say the same thing about someone, you might want to listen. It is probably true. A person gains a reputation over time by doing the same thing to many people. A reputation is a good thing to pay attention to. The odds are that if someone is repeatedly bad to other people, he will be bad to you.

Meanwhile, a good reputation is an encouraging sign. Someone who gains a reputation as being honest or nice is usually really that way. However, don't rely on reputation alone. Someone may be good at pulling the wool over everyone's eyes. You might be able to read bad things in him that no one else can. Trust your gut in this scenario. Just because everyone else likes someone does not mean that you should, too. Sometimes the most upstanding citizens are hiding very dark secrets and underneath their honest reputations they have dirty souls.

Reading People for Clues

First Impressions

First impressions are typically accurate. You should listen to your gut. Your subconscious mind is adept at picking out clues about people that your rational mind cannot possibly pick up on. Your gut will tell you the most accurate information about someone right off of the bat.

After you make a first impression, you may try to rationalize it. You may try to explain away negative feelings as poor judgment or jealousy. You may think that you read a person wrong. While these are vaguely possible, you will usually find out that your first impression was right in the end.

A good example is when you first meet a woman that you would like to be friends with. But your gut reaction to her is that she is not very nice. You decide to give her a chance since everyone else likes her and you get along after a while. After a while, however, you realize that all she does is say mean things about other people. Or she may betray you after years of friendship.

Your first impression is often all you have in business and situations like speed dating. So trust it. Your first impression is most likely correct, so act on it if you do not have time to get to know the person further.

Red Flags

There are some major red flags that automatically tell you that someone is toxic. When you observe these traits or habits in someone, you know that someone is not good to be around. Run away when you spot these red flags. Do not try to somehow rationalize or justify these traits, as they are serious signs of underlying emotional issues or sociopath.

Easy to Anger

A person who is easily ignited has anger problems. One day you will probably be the victim of his anger if you are not careful. Therefore, you should avoid people who are angered easily. A history of violence is one sign that a person is easy to anger. Another sign is if he seems to demonstrate an angry posture. He will talk about fighting people or getting angry. He will immediately appear angry over the tiniest setbacks, such as his food being late at a restaurant.

Blaming Others

Right off the bat, you will notice if someone frequently blames others for what is wrong in his life. He will tell you all about how he is a victim. He will complain about how his ex-spouse cheated on him and brought about the divorce, he will blame getting fired recently on the fact that his former boss is just a huge jerk, and he will blame his recent car accident on the other stupid driver.

Nothing will ever be his fault. He will claim that everyone else is responsible for his problems. And he will have plenty of problems to talk about. He will always be a victim. Someone who plays the victim will probably one day accuse you of doing something wrong to him. He will never see how he is at fault. He will certainly never own up to his own bad actions or offer you any kind of apology.

Constant Complaining

A person who is very negative will just ooze that negativity through his speech. He will constantly complain about everything. It will appear as if the world is against him and nothing in life is good or worth doing. Just being around this person too long will make you feel depressed.

Sadly, many people are like this. They only see the bad in life. You can assume that a person like this will only bring you down. You will never be able to lighten someone like this up because he chooses to stay in a depressed mood.

Gossiping and Two-Facing

Some gossip is just human nature. Once you know someone well, a little bit of gossip now and then is normal. It is not a warning sign.

But when you first meet someone, the first thing you hear should not be a bunch of gossip about other people. A person who sits there talking about everyone else has a gossiping problem. He is obviously two-faced. Don't be fooled and think that you are the only one that he gossips to. Once you leave the room, he will start gossiping about you.

If someone gossips a lot, you want to watch what you say around him. You do not want to reveal too much, or it will become public information in two seconds.

You also do not want to let his negativity sour you against other people. He will try to make you hate everyone else with the juicy, horrible details that he shares, but remember that gossip is rarely true. Even if it is, you do not have to be a part of this gossip's drama. Women have the worst reputations as gossips. But men can be just as bad. Anyone who talks about other people a lot is a gossip. Be careful around such people.

Lacking Compassion

Have you ever met someone who laughs when other people fall? He seems to get some sick satisfaction from the suffering of others. Even if he doesn't snicker at other people, he never demonstrates any remorse or compassion.

When he speaks about other people, he uses very callous and cold language. When you point out someone's bad luck, for instance, he will snort and say that it is the person's own fault. This is the sign of a sociopath or psychopath. This person is very dangerous and certainly not the type of person that you want in your life.

The average person is capable of at least some compassion in conversation. He will feel bad when you mention that you are going through tough times or when someone falls, for instance.

Someone who does not show any compassion and just ignores you or offers a callous remark when you say something that calls for compassion is not someone that you should associate with. If you do associate with this person, never expect him to show you compassion when you need it.

Things to Read

What He is Driven By?

People are driven by various things. They will usually show what drives them by talking about it. For example, someone might say that he wants to go out to pick up chicks. Obviously sex drives him. Someone who frequently talks about money and making money is driven by financial security and wealth. Someone who talks about socializing a lot is an extrovert who is driven by having social interaction.

What drives a person can indicate what he wants from you. Read a person's language to gather clues about what he wants in life. His drive can indicate why he is seeking any sort of relationship with you, either professionally or personally. It also indicates what is important to him. If your goals align with his, then a relationship is a great idea. Otherwise, you may want to steer clear of this person.

What Feeds His Ego

Watch a person's ego to find out what feeds it. A lot of people are fed by accomplishments, such as making money or finishing a tough marathon. Some people are fed by flattery and being the object of desire. Some people are fed by sex and interactions with the opposite sex. What feeds someone's ego is apparent by what he talks about the most and what makes him smile.

Also, watch his responses to life situations. If a member of the opposite sex flirts with someone and his or her ego blossoms, you can assume that he or she has low self-esteem and requires lots of sexual attention to feel good. If he brags about his boat and other material possessions, you can tell that material success is what makes him feel complete.

If someone has a fragile ego that is fed by superficial things like material possessions and sexual attention, you can be sure that he has little confidence. The issues that come with insecurity are thus probably prevalent in this person. He will also do things to satisfy his own ego, and will chase after things and make stupid decisions just to keep his ego buoyed. Expect vices in someone like this.

But if someone's ego is fed by more solid things, such as his own accomplishments or the love of his family, then he is probably a secure and reliable person with healthy confidence and wholesome interests. You can trust someone like this to be a more solid companion in business or in your personal life.

What Stresses Him Out

Watch out for someone's stressors. Everyone has a source of stress. What a person complains about the most usually indicates what causes him the most emotional stress. If he complains about family, communication, commitment, and not always getting his way or not feeling loved may cause him stress.

If he complains about work, his line of work and the tasks that he must do are probably not well-suited to his personality. If he seems to get quiet or upset in large crowds, you can assume that large crowds are not his forte. Knowing what stresses someone out is very useful information. You can learn what to avoid doing around someone. You can become more sensitive to what someone does not like and also to situations that a person does not function well in. This is great information to know if you hire someone to work for you or if you begin dating someone.

What Pleases Him

People will go on and on about what makes them happy. You will most likely find out what makes someone happy relatively early in conversation. But you can also look for clues in what makes someone smile or what someone fixates on with dilated pupils.

This is also useful to know. You learn what you can do to please someone. This can make you a better lover, friend, or even employer and co-worker.

How Does He Behave Under Stress

How someone handles stress says a lot about how he will treat you when things get hard. Life can throw a lot of challenges your way, so you usually want people around who can handle stress well. If a stressful situation arises and someone literally falls apart or gets fiercely angry, just know that he is probably not a reliable friend during times of stress.

He is also not a good prospect in a stressful line of business. On the other hand, if he is able to remain calm and collected under stress, he is someone that you can rely on in the future.

Chapter 8: The art of reading any kind of person

Decoding people's facial expressions is one skill that you cannot afford to miss out. With such a skill, you get information about people which the average person wouldn't have. Very few individuals have this kind of skill. No wonder we have too many heartbreaks and broken deals. Remember that 80% of emotions are shown by the face.

So, if you get to properly decode the facial expressions in advance, you will highlight behaviors that signal danger in the near future. This chapter takes you through the various ways in which you can become better at reading people's facial expressions.

#1: Differentiate between observing and looking

Most people look at others' faces, thinking they are observing them. Even though both observation and looking is done with the use of eyes, the two are completely different. They are mistakenly used to mean the other but that ought to change. Looking is when you see others without the intent of getting to know more than what is visible to the eye. You do not try to derive meaning out of the actions done by others neither do you try to commit anything to the brain.

Observing has to do with seeing the actions performed by people and keeping the visions in mind so that you can make meaning out of them, posing questions. You perform deductions, that is, separating vital details from the unimportant ones, utilizing your careful observation to conclude. Make sure that you know the two are different so that you do not waste time looking at people thinking you are observing them. In fact, in looking you will end up awkwardly staring others and it may even earn you a smack in the face.

#2: Be curious

For you to decode one's facial expression, you must have some form of curiosity towards him/her. It is this curiosity that drives you to dedicate your time observing them. It is human nature to pay attention to what interests them.

If you develop negative attitudes towards others, chances are you may not observe them diligently. That calls for an effort on your part to prevent your feelings or emotions from getting in the way of your observation. Even if you do not like somebody but you still have to observe them, make sure that you keep the dislike at bay or else you will achieve nothing.

Identify something that you find to be intriguing about others and curiously purpose to exploit it further. Understand that we all learn from each other and so even if they appear to be different, appreciate that and continue observing them.

Is there somebody you do not like but they still have friends who are so fond of them? Curiosity would drive you into wanting to know why they have the following despite you despising them. If you spot some differences between you and others, curiosity would lead you into wanting to know why the differences exist.

#3: Say NO to judgment

Being judgmental is the number one thing that will block you from making effective observation of people. When you judge others, you feed your brain with the wrong information and block it from getting facts.

For a good people observer, neutrality is prioritized. Observations are free of personal feelings since such elements are comprised of biasness. When you involve prejudices, preconceived notions and personal feelings, you are not able to see what is there. You only get to see what you want to see.

A good people observer knows how to ignore their personal feelings so that they can feed their brains with the right details for analysis. To avoid being judgmental as you go about observing others, begin by taking a step back. Refrain from trying to enter into the other person's life and let them just be themselves. Do not try to make conclusions about whatever they do.

Rather than thinking of a negative experience you had with them or saw them perform, see them for who they are – a person. If they drive a certain car, do not look at them in a certain way just because you associate the car with a particular social class. When you are neutral, you are able to see people clearly.

#4: Stare more where possible

There is something about staring at people that makes you get finer details that had been previously concealed from your eyes. One of the ways to observe people is to stare at them and the things they like doing, but you must make sure you are not within the framework that might define you as being 'creepy.'

We tend to encode more information from what the eyes sees as opposed to what is spoken or written. Stare as much as necessary for the eyes to pick relevant data and send it to the brain for analysis.

Staring at people can be a tricky engagement. Even from your own perspective, if you see somebody just staring at you, you will feel kind of awkward or may even want to react violently. Thus, your staring should be a purposeful stare but one that is concealed.

If you can get your hands to videos involving such people and uploaded online, the better. You could lock yourself in a room and stare at the people in videos until you get what you are looking for. While in public, control the urge to stare to levels that let you get basic information.

#5: Avoid distractions

The reason as to why you may not perform a good observation is because you are distracted. As you go about your observation, a What Sapp notification on your smartphone could force you to lose focus on what you were doing. The distractions are all over us, whether it's your to-do list, music or cell phones. The best way to focus on people observation is to eliminate these distractions.

Remove your headphones as you interact with other people. Allow yourself to hear the surrounding sounds and probably what others are saying (but do not appear to be eavesdropping). If you are watching a video that has the person whom you are observing, concentrate on it as you listen to any conversations held. Rather than watching mindlessly, pay attention. Think about what they wore and why they acted in a particular way.

Chapter 9: Tips on how to be a better reader

Reading other people is not all about what you can do for yourself. It's also about what you can do for other people.

You will learn how to set people at their ease, tell when they are in need of something that they can't or won't tell you about and, perhaps most importantly, how to understand them and their needs, hopes and desires.

There is no greater gift you can offer to another human being than understanding and acceptance of who they are and willingness to provide what they are looking for.

Free you're Judgment

There are many things that can cloud your judgment when reading people. Biases, intimidation, and sexual attraction are just some of the things that can make you choose to ignore your gut and misread someone. You may think that someone's harsh actions are admirable if you admire the person, while their actions would appear despicable if you did not admire them. Do not let anything cloud your judgment.

Men are more likely to judge pretty young women less harshly. They let pretty young women get away with disrespectful behavior in hopes of winning their favor. If you are attracted to someone, you are more likely to ignore red flags about the person. Try to look past sexual attraction. Understand that there are plenty of attractive people in the world, so fixating on one person's attractiveness are not necessary. You just need to view an attractive person more objectively. Try to focus on his or her character as a separate thing from his or her looks.

Status or certain jobs can also make you admire someone. But understand that someone is not perfect just because of his or her status. Do not let someone's status intimidate you or bamboozle you. In fact, they probably got to where they are today by being cruel to others. Read their character separately from their status or work. Being in your own emotional funk can really distort your judgment, too. When you are emotionally down, you may be harsher to judge others in your state of bitterness. You may also be more vulnerable to kind actions from others. Unfortunately, manipulators are great at spotting when you are upset and offering a kind action in order to gain favor with you. Do not let your emotional state make you vulnerable in judgment.

Emotional wounds can make it hard for you to trust people. This is especially true after you been through a divorce or bad break-up. As a result, you might judge the gender that you are attracted to unfairly. You may instantly dislike all people of that gender. Do not be so quick to write off people that you do not know. Use your scars as lessons to read people who remind you of those that have hurt you in the past, but do not make the mistake of thinking that the entire gender is bad. Give individuals a chance. Try to read them, for who they are, not who your ex was.

Don't Just Base it Off of Behavior

Many people make the mistake of trying to read people off of behavior alone. But often behavior offers an incomplete and inaccurate picture. You must consider someone's biases, mood, and even the context of the situation. Often, you cannot know all of this information, so don't even attempt to read someone based off of behavior alone. Sometimes behavior is inaccurate because it is fake. Many people are great at creating a façade. They appear totally normal and upstanding, while hiding their horrendous internal flaws. Think of most serial killers. Often they go to work, keep nice houses, and look like totally normal people. The world is shocked when they are finally caught with a basement full of hacked up bodies and torture devices. Sexual deviants who get caught watching child porn are often politicians and businessmen with great jobs and totally normal outside appearances. While these examples are extreme, many people are adept at hiding their bad personalities under totally normal behavior. Therefore, you cannot base judgments off of the outward behavior of others, as this behavior can be faked and misleading.

Create a Baseline

Try to gauge a baseline of someone's normal behavior. Watch for unusual mannerisms that a person often displays. Quirks and habits that you frequently observe in someone over time form the person's baseline. A baseline does not take long to form once you become more adept at reading people with practice. FBI profilers will usually gather this information within the first fifteen seconds of meeting a person.

From this baseline, you are able to tell when someone is behaving abnormally. When someone is behaving abnormally, you can determine that something is going on. Perhaps the person is lying or is upset about something. It is difficult to start a baseline on someone if you do not have a chance to observe him over a period of time and you are not yet adept at reading people in just a few seconds.

Therefore, it is a good idea to watch for really odd behavior. Behavior that stands out as unusual may be a quirk or it may be a sign of something more ominous, such as deception. You may want to ask other people who know the person well if this behavior is normal for him. If you can't do that, then you simply must rely on your gut. But do not rely too much on behavior to form judgments about people.

You can start a baseline just by asking someone how they are doing today. Watch how the person reacts. From there, you can determine what his or her normal mannerisms are.

The more you talk, the more you can gather about the person's baseline. Does his eye tic often? Does he often gesticulate with his hands? Does he stutter normally, or is he normally articulate? Also gauge the speed with which he speaks in normal conversation and the tone and pitch of his voice. You must establish a baseline in order to tell when someone is behaving inconsistently. In addition, a baseline lets you know how a person is in normal settings.

If a person is typically nervous, you can decide if you want to be around someone who is frequently nervous and therefore probably insecure with social anxiety. If a person is typically rude and blunt, you can determine if you want to deal with that kind of behavior in the future.

Infer Things from the Initial Reaction

Of course, strangers tend to be tense in their initial behavior toward you because they do not know you well. But a person's initial reaction to you indicates a lot of information about how he feels about himself and how he feels about other people. This initial reaction shows the hang-ups he may have and the guard that he puts up to protect himself or the façade that he erects to charm people that he meets for the first time. As a result, this reaction says a lot about who he is as a person and the things that you may expect from him as you get to know him better. If he is initially rude, for instance, he may thaw and become nicer toward you, but you know that at heart he has his guard up against new people.

You can then wonder why he has his guard up. He is probably a sensitive and insecure person with a lot of emotional baggage; he feels that he has to act tough and careless in order to avoid getting hurt. Particularly articulate and charming people usually have a lot to hide. They are great at being around people and hiding who they really are. They have designed behavior that is intended to hook people. Very charming behavior is often indicative of manipulative and deceptive personalities.

A person who is overly nervous usually has social anxiety and is rife with insecurities. This person will probably get more comfortable with you over time. However, you may want to avoid trusting him too much. As a general rule, people who are insecure are not reliable and will act in ways that are not always appropriate. Insecure people tend to have trust issues and they will act out in ways that are hurtful because they believe that they are not good enough. You are not responsible for the insecurities of another person, so don't allow such a person to burden you with his problems and doubts.

A person who acts too calm is probably also a sufferer of social anxiety. However, he is adept at projecting calmness to hide how nervous he is. Become suspicious of people who are just "too chill." Also watch for people who only want to talk about themselves. People who are obsessed with themselves and don't even try to ask you questions about yourself are typically very selfish. This behavior will not change with time.

Another behavior that will not change with time is someone who is negative, even on your first meeting. People like this are very toxic and will simply try to drag you down. A person who talks about others shamelessly when he first meets you is also probably a chronic gossip. It is not normal for someone to start gossiping when he first meets you. Positivity and enthusiasm are great signs in a person that you have just met. However, if someone talks too much of a big game and brags overly much, you can assume that this person is trying to impress you or even make up for something that he feels that he is lacking. Mild positivity and enthusiasm is a great sign, but being overly enthusiastic is not.

Confidence and assurance of one's self is a good sign in a stranger. A person who is willing to introduce himself to you, look you in the eye, and talk to you is usually secure in himself.

He has developed good social skills and hence might be a more sensitive friend, lover, or work associate. While you want to be wary of people who are too smooth and charming, someone who acts normal yet confident is usually a good person to know.

Ask Pointed Questions

If you want to get to know someone, feel free to ask him questions about himself. He will probably volunteer a lot of the information that you want to know. You don't even have to ask him things to find out a lot of information about who he is as a person, what he likes, and what he is looking for from his association with you. This is why you should be a good listener, which I cover in the next chapter.

But if he does not volunteer what you want to know, then ask. It is best to ask pointed questions and to not be vague. If you are vague, you run the risk of miscommunication. As an adult, there is no use or time for games anymore. You know that you cannot be a mind reader and neither can anyone else. So ask what you want to know without shame.

You do not want appear like you are interrogating someone. Asking rapid-fire questions can really put a person off. Asking overly personal questions about someone's life, family, or personality is also off-putting. But do not be afraid to ask general, socially acceptable questions whenever there is a break in the conversation. Monitor a person in how he answers your questions. Since you have already more or less established a good baseline, you can tell when there are inconsistencies in his responses. If his gestures, tone, pitch, or eye contact suddenly shifts away from his baseline, then you can tell that he is not being truthful or that a question makes him uncomfortable for some reason. You can change the subject or pursue it more, depending on your goal in communication with him.

Word Choice is Important

How a person talks indicates a lot about what he is feeling and thinking. Listen for key words that indicate his intentions and his basic state of mind. he words that he chooses say a lot about how he is as a human being and what he is really feeling at the moment. If you are meeting someone for the first time, remember that the initial meeting speaks volumes about who a person is inside. How he chooses to speak to you right off the bat indicates a lot about who he is generally.

Someone who uses very harsh, aggressive language is an aggressive person or else he is currently in an angry mood. You never want someone to show you anger when you first meet; this indicates that the person may have an anger management problem. Someone who uses very vague wording is possibly passive aggressive and trying to skirt around a hard subject. This type of person is not able to be direct. Expect games and behavior like shirking responsibility.

If this person wrongs you, he will probably never admit to it and apologize. If he has a problem with you, he will probably never tell you to your face, but rather will hint about it or tell everyone else how he feels except for you. Another troubling sign is when someone repeatedly says sorry or seems to take the blame for things. This type of person is very sinecure and blames him for everything.

Someone who uses conceited language, such as bragging about how he just won "another" award, indicates how proud he is of himself. Watch for people who brag too much about themselves. These people are usually narcissistic and egotistical or else they are over compensating for feelings of inadequacy. A person who uses very critical language is probably an overly judgmental person or a perfectionist. Watch for someone who nitpicks everything. This is a trait that will not lessen with time. If anything, it will only grow worse with time.

Most people use "I" terms more frequently than any other. This is not a troubling sign, but someone who uses more "we" terms is a better team player who is looking to collaborate with you. Someone who uses more "you" terms is focused on you. This can be a great sign that someone is focused on pleasing you and getting to know you, or else it can be a worrisome sign that someone is trying to manipulate you. Watch for other word choices in order to tell the difference. If someone is asking you about what you like or who you are, then that is usually a sign that he wants to get to know you or find out how to best please you.

This is a great sign in a date, a new friend, or a person that you are thinking about hiring for a service. But if he seems to be fishing for pertinent information with overly personal questions, if he keeps trying to find ways that he can commiserate with you so that you will confide in him, or if he is using fancy language and flattery to make you feel ingratiated and charmed by him, then that is a bad sign that he is trying to get an emotional hook into you in order to manipulate you.

A good sign that someone is being shifty is vague language. Someone who refuses to answer yes or no questions is probably lying. Someone who uses confusing language is probably deliberately creating a sort of mirage of vagueness in order to hide something.

What is Unsaid Says a Lot?

Studies suggest that ninety-three percent of human communication is unspoken. Since this is such a huge topic, I have dedicated an entire chapter to reading the tonality, body language, eye contact, and other nonverbal cues of other people for clues about what they are really trying to say.

Chapter 10: Identifying different Behavioral Traits

Detecting deceit will give you the rare opportunity to choose your associates wisely without having to say a word. The body goes into an immense ball of anxiety when a person lies. The trained eye will be able to detect these small variances that occur. Although words may speak their version of the truth, the body never lies. Deceit is the act of covering up the way you truly feel through seeking control.

Oftentimes, that control is executed in a sloppy manner, thus leading to dominant cues that signal deceit. Whether it's a large lie or a little white lie, the results of dishonesty come with a variety of consequences. Essentially, people lie as a subconscious form of protection. They are either hiding their negative behavior or protecting their reputations. Even when used to exaggerate a story, they may be attempting to protect the fact that their life is truly boring. They want others to find them enjoyable. Thus, various lies are told.

One organization divides deceit into four categories of explanation and uses:

Anxiety- seeking to hide the fact that they are nervous

Control- gestures or smiles that are forced or a grand attempt to stop the body from moving

Distraction- Frequent pausing or bodily actions in between answers is that person's attempt to distract you from their lie. By acting out these grand gestures, they believe they are making their stories believable.

Persuasion- Deceit may stem from wanting someone to carry out an action which will result in the liar's favor.

Joseph Tecce, a researcher at Boston College, exposed the six reasons why individuals lie in addition to their respective character traits:

1. Protective Lies: This protects the reputation of the liar or even the victim from undue harm. They seek to keep their social status by not revealing true behavior.

2. Heroic Liars: These individuals will lie in an attempt to uphold the greater good. For example, a popular episode of **Sex and the City** portrayed Carrie and her friend, Stanford, at a mixer. Stanford was interested in a handsome man across the room. He asked Carrie to go and find out if the man was gay or straight. She approached him and let him know of Stanford's interest. The man looked at Stanford from across the room in utter repulsion. As Carrie went back to her hopeful friend, she told him that the handsome man was straight. She wanted to protect her friend's self-esteem by not revealing the truth.

3. Playful Liars: Playful liars accentuate their stories in order to provide a means of entertainment for listeners.

4. Ego Liars: Ego liars will cover mistakes in order to protect their reputations or status.

5. Gainful Liars: These are people who lie for personal gain.

6. Malicious Liars: These are the individuals who are out to seek revenge and harm others due to psychological challenges.

Many individuals are so crafty at lying; they have mastered the art of concealing their body movements. Sociopaths and psychopaths alike are so deranged; they feel no emotional connection to the lies.

It is quite difficult to detect their inaccuracies because they are so connected to the lies. They may even begin to believe the lies. When considering the deceit of mentally stable individuals, however, there may be concrete reasons behind their excessive lying. Let's consider a few signs of a deceitful person and consider their traits. The head can offer a slight indication of a person beginning to lie. When being asked a question, a liar tends to quickly move their head prior to responding. Interestingly, the face holds many of the truest signs of deception.

We express honest emotions through the theory of timing. Researchers have found that, naturally, we hold our expressions between one and four seconds. When a person is lying or faking an emotion, the expression is usually held for a longer period of time.

In addition, their symmetrical alignment can play a huge role in detecting insincerity. To tell if a person is being honest, notice the purest emotions are evenly distributed throughout the face. However, a liar will typically express their emotions on one side dominantly.

Our speech and body movements should complement each other. So if a person is telling you how beautiful you look while frowning and crossing their arms, it is safe to conclude that they aren't genuine. Excessive body movements are often associated with nervousness. Naturally, though, the body engages in slight movements even without the presence of anxiety. However, Dr. Leanne Brinke, professor of the Haas School of Business, indicates that a person who remains as still as a statue should be further examined.

Have you ever noticed that when catching someone in a lie, their body tends to freeze almost like a deer caught in headlights? Essentially, they are shocked that their behavior has been caught. At that moment, they have lost all control, and they feel exposed. In order to gain some form of control, they clench their body. It is also key to notice where their hands go when being confronted. Do they cover their mouths? Throats? Chests? By providing this subtle distraction, they are protecting themselves from the truth.

They have no intention of telling the truth, so they are, in effect, covering areas of the body that assist with communication. In addition, verbal cues also point towards deception. Excessive repeating, stuttering, and clearing of the throat are key signs of nervousness. They are desperately trying to buy time to respond. Traditionally, the eyes have been closely associated with deceit. Previously, we spoke about the connection between dilation and interest. When we see something we love or are attracted to, our eyes dilate. When in a relationship, a key indicator of a loss of interest rests in the pupils. When you ask your mate if your outfit looks great, they may say it looks awesome, but the pupils tell the truth. Excessive darting of the eyes or an avoidance of eye contact signifies some level of deceit.

The person may be attempting to put on the demeanor of aggression, but they refuse to look at another's eyes. Are they truly as tough as they say they are? Interestingly, the right side of the brain controls auditory processing, big picture ideas, and decision making. When a person darts their eyes downward and towards the right, they are attempting to envision something, perhaps visiting a place they have never been.

They may look down and to the right when thinking about what it's like to live there. When someone is lying, notice how they may repeat this same motion.

Interestingly, they are attempting to envision something that didn't occur rather than recall a memory. The body is also a clear indicator of deceit. You may notice the person's breathing patterns significantly speed up. Their chest could move faster, and their breathing becomes louder. Their shoulders and elbows are stiffly raised. This movement represents being caught, as seen depicted in cartoons. The robber may inadvertently stop in their tracks with their shoulders raised. They are trying to protect themselves by growing defensive. Psychics and spiritual healers utilize exposed palms to reveal truth.

Although controversial, many readers analyze the open palms to detect repressed emotions, predict future occurrences, and decode personality. When a person is lying, those palms of truth are suddenly closed and facing away from the subject. It's a subconscious way of not wanting to reveal their truth. Although detecting liars is an essential tool to have, simply noticing a liar isn't productive. Effective communication in conjunction with understanding can help to reveal lies and reach solutions.

key behavior that indicates deception/lie

Many individuals are so crafty at lying; they have mastered the art of concealing their body movements. Sociopaths and psychopaths alike are so deranged; they feel no emotional connection to the lies. It is quite difficult to detect their inaccuracies because they are so connected to the lies. They may even begin to believe the lies. When considering the deceit of mentally stable individuals, however, there may be concrete reasons behind their excessive lying. Let's consider a few signs of a deceitful person and consider their traits.

The head can offer a slight indication of a person beginning to lie. When being asked a question, a liar tends to quickly move their head prior to responding. Interestingly, the face holds many of the truest signs of deception. We express honest emotions through the theory of timing. Researchers have found that, naturally, we hold our expressions between one and four seconds. When a person is lying or faking an emotion, the expression is usually held for a longer period of time. In addition, their symmetrical alignment can play a huge role in detecting insincerity.

To tell if a person is being honest, notice the purest emotions are evenly distributed throughout the face. However, a liar will typically express their emotions on one side dominantly. Our speech and body movements should complement each other. So if a person is telling you how beautiful you look while frowning and crossing their arms, it is safe to conclude that they aren't genuine.

key behavior that signal attraction/trust

These are a few subtle cues to look out for when spotting romantic interest. These clues are almost unnoticeable, and you really need to concentrate on seeing them. They may not seem important, but once you identify what they are, they will change the game forever.

Below are a few subtle cues that imply attraction:

- Dilated pupils
- The nostrils of men slightly flare
- Men have the tendency to touch their lips or chin
- Women have the tendency to touch their hair or face

Subtle cues that portray disinterest are:

- Men keep their distance when standing
- Men keep their arms closed around themselves
- Women are distracted or fidgety
- Women hold their purses in front of them

key behavior that signal insecurity and the signs that show a lack of confidence

Sometimes, a person will shuffle along, without any rhythm or flowing motion to his movement. Other times, he walks with his head bowed due to lack of confidence. If you notice these signs in a person you are dealing with, make an effort to offer a compliment to the individual.

A compliment works wonders in boosting the individual's confidence. If you are having a discussion with him, ask him some questions; most shy people have a lot of wisdom and insight to share, they only need to be asked questions so that they may open up.

Chapter 11: How to set up the dialogue to analyze the person

In order to properly analyze others, it is important to seek understanding with your own body movements. In social settings, the way we position our body can be the difference between making friends and repelling them.

Since we cannot see our body movements as well as others, it's important to become in tune with your feelings and perception. Many times, we may not even realize the silent signals we are giving off. Sure, we have the ability to speak our emotions, but we all know that the truth is seldom spoken. Science has proven that we emit energy that can be detected, and is even contagious. When you're inner energy is feeling tired or bored, your outward appearance will give evidence of that energy despite how "excited" you say you are.

Technology has given us the grand opportunity to display rejection with the simple glance down at the phone. For example, when a friend is telling you a story that you are 100 percent not interested in, likely you will reach for your phone and begin scrolling.

Your words are saying, "Uh-huh," occasionally, but your demeanor speaks volumes. You may believe you are listening when really you are showing outward disdain for your friend. This sign is often taken as disrespect and could create distance in the friendship. Another common sign is the crossing of the arms. In social occasions, this can be translated as, "I don't want to be here." When in reality, you could simply be cold. Since this is what you are exhibiting, others are naturally going to view you as unapproachable.

Do you find yourself doing this quite often? Crossing of the arms is another form of protection. It is almost likened to a comfort mechanism that we do when in an uncomfortable situation. This can be attributed to a form of social anxiety and inner insecurity. Sure, you may be the most inviting person in the room, but you are not aware of that yet.

Your inner, primal voice is activating your fight or flight response. You may be subconsciously uncomfortable with your outfit, afraid of others' opinions, or even fearful of talking to people. The importance of becoming aware of your deeper desires will work wonders towards your body language.

Another instance occurs during one-on-one communication. Do you notice your eyes drifting during a conversation? Or even your hand being placed on your face while someone is talking? This signals disinterest and could be extremely disrespectful to the person talking. In turn, your friend could become upset with you without you even realizing it. Flirtation can be a fine and tricky art because many of the signals of genuine interest and attraction are often intertwined. For example, a young man was engaging in a conversation with a married woman at a public event. She was talking to him about a job opportunity she had available in her department.

Being recently laid off from his job, naturally, the man was excited! He began to shift his body towards her as he leaned his head in. His eyes never left hers, and he had a slight smile on his face.

Upon noticing, the woman's husband grew increasingly alert to their conversation. From the outside, all he saw was this young man, leaning in towards his wife with a smile. Unbeknownst to him, the situation was far from flirtatious. This is a clear indicator of how our body language deeply affects the way people view us. When engaging in that conversation, the young man was extremely interested in the possible job opportunity, not the married woman. However, his body language signaled attraction.

The importance of being aware of how your body is positioned when speaking to others is a subliminal sign of respect. One fantastic way to become aware of your body motions is to remember the three W's: who, what, and where. Let's consider them one at a time.

Who

When speaking with another person, it's key to remember who you are engaging with. Is it a close friend of the opposite sex? Is it your manager or maybe even an older person? In all of these instances, the way you position your body means everything. Take, for example, speaking with your manager. Do you find yourself naturally crossing your arms when he or she approaches you? This could be your way of protecting yourself against their authority, or you may actually dislike your manager.

However, you want to keep your job and even appear interested in what he or she has to say. This instance is when acting and awareness play a major role. When you see your manager coming, the butterflies may ensue. You may even become a bit clammy in the hands. Instead of allowing that feeling to overpower you, simply acknowledge it, and let it be. Don't try to manipulate the feeling as that causes further anxiety.

Rather, acknowledge it, and place your hands by your side with open palms. Try your best to breathe and remain comfortable. Position your back upright with your shoulders aligned. Create an opening demeanor that opens the door for conversation.

What

When engaging in a conversation, try to feel what your body is doing. Are your hands clenched in a fist? Do you feel your face tightening as if you're displeased?

When you become aware of what your body does when engaging in a conversation, you will be able to control those muscles. One vital question you can ask yourself is, "What is my body telling others right now?" By doing so, you can immediately change the way others perceive you.

Where

It's especially important to be cognizant of where you are when speaking to others. Oftentimes, certain atmospheres may warrant specific behavior. For example, during a blind date, it would be quite rude to scrunch your forehead and brows in disgust at your date's appearance. Sure, they may not be what you expected, but you never want to display your inner emotions. In addition, you wouldn't walk into a funeral with a big smile and open arms.

Even if you barely knew the deceased, that demeanor may appear heartless to the grieving family. Making the connection between what your body is doing and remembering where you are is imperative for your reputation. Body awareness is key to navigating your world. It is defined as "the sense that we have of our own bodies." It is an understanding of the parts that make up one's body, where they are located, how they feel, and even what they can do.

Certain activities such as yoga and Pilates assist with connecting the bridge between the body and mind. When engaging in these exercises, you are mentally aware of the positioning of your body. You have full control over your balance which strengthens your mental and physical muscles. Engaging in these activities on a regular basis can assist with understanding your body movements. This will come in handy when evaluating what your body is doing in social settings.

To practice your own proprioception exercise at home, begin by balancing on one foot. What are your arms doing? Your fingers? Do you feel a tingle in your opposing leg? Become engrossed in how your body is working together to keep you balanced. By repeating this simple exercise daily, you'll begin to notice the movements of even the smallest parts of your body.

In order to fully understand the body language of others, you have to become connected with your personal movements. Body language is more than just reading movements. It's attributing a deeper meaning towards body posture that can speak volumes into a person's emotions.

Chapter 12: Tips and tricks to fake your body language

Some people have just too much ego that they wouldn't allow their facial expressions to be shown. When clearly a particular matter has hurt them and that they are undergoing immense pain in the inside, their big egos would not let them reveal such details.

These are the kinds of people who suffer in silence and within a couple of days; you may get information that they did something more harmful – suicide for example. There is also this category of people who hide their facial expressions, not because they want to do so, but because they just do not know how to solve negative emotions.

As negativity builds up from the inside and starts to show in the face, they soon device ways to hide any form of negative expressions to lock you out from analyzing them. They want to look happy when in real sense they are sad. They want you to see that they are having a good time but in reality there is a sickness or school fees issue that has been stressing them for months now. We all know that negative emotions can lead to frowning on one's face, which essentially makes them not so approachable or appealing. Thus, in an attempt to retain their attractiveness, they conceal any form of negative facial expression which would have otherwise confronted them. In other cases, some people may hide their facial expressions just so as to please. These are the people who believe in the philosophy that what you do not know cannot hurt you. Their idea is that when they keep some information from you, you may still have a happy life.

Thus, when they speak to you, they will struggle to build a certain kind of facial expression which conveys the message that all is well while in real sense that is further from the truth. Let's say for example one of your best friends gets some bad news from the doctor that they have cancer and that they have only a few years with you.

They love you so much and know how much such news could be devastating to you. In order to save you all the pain, they may choose to struggle with the pain on their own, believing that provided you do not know about it, you will have a happy life. Whenever they tell stories with you, they will do their best not to let you into the inside. From their facial expressions, they will be smiling for you whereas only they know the agony they are experiencing. You have the responsibility of decoding this so that you get the message they are trying to lock inside.

5 Signs someone is being fake: How to tell they are faking facial expressions

1. Taking deep breath

This is a technique that seems to be universal amongst all people who express untrue facial expressions. You will often see them appear to be unrelated and continuously breathe in and out heavily in the midst of their explanations over a matter you just asked.

Because they know that for you to believe the facial expression they just wore to impress you, they have to appear calm. That is what the deep breathes are meant to do – take in more oxygen so that they can recollect their composure and be cool. If you are not keen enough on the breathing pattern, their faces may appear calm to you and succeed in the deception.

2. Putting up a fake smile

A smile never says that someone is happy at all times. Someone who smiles and has a bubbly look on their face can win hearts and affection. As a result, many assume that with just the right smile, they will be able to hide their feelings like anger or sadness. But a fake smile will always be fake. It may convince some people at the first glance but a keen individual will soon realize this smile is fake. How well you know the individual could guide you into distinguishing between the smile they just put up and their real happy smile. But even if you do not know them that well, their inability to sustain the smile will eventually prove it fake.

3. Trying not to supporting the head

There is something about 'cooked' facial expressions that makes the head heavy. People who understand the technique of hiding facial expressions know this. Thus, they always try to make sure that their head is held up high to better deceive you.

When you are keen on them, there will be these occasions when they can no longer hold the head up and end up burying the face in their palms for some seconds before realizing that they may show you that they are lying. Careful analysis of the struggles not to support the head could reveal to you that they are faking their facial expression.

4. Struggling to relax the face

A relaxed face can easily build up a deceiving facial expression. For example, your son may have committed an offense in school and they come to report the matter to you, hoping to come out as victims. If your first glance on their faces shows them as being relaxed, you could actually be deceived and even get on the wrong side with the teachers. However, if you saw their faces were not relaxed even before they started the explanation, you can tell right away that there must be a problem somewhere.

When you speak to someone and at one time their face is relaxed and at the other one it is not, that is a sign of a problem. Within a few minutes their face could be straight while at another it is steel and acting like a tough guy. This shows that they may have tried to relax it up to a certain point when they could do it no more. There is something here; take a deep look at their faces and you shall see it.

5. *Silent lip movements*

To be calm, some people speak to themselves. They may say something like "Calm down, you can do this. Just stay cool." If you are not careful, they may actually succeed in being calm and creating a falsified facial expression. Through a keen look at the lip movements, you may tell that the person has more things that they are hiding under their facial expressions.

Conclusion

Successfully analyzing others can be a vast and complex area of study, and a seemingly daunting pursuit for one to take on if you do not know what you are looking for. However it really is just about breaking down the various elements before putting them back together to complete the behavior puzzle. To build the picture of what somebody is really thinking.

You have to start with yourself, the reason why humans act the way we do to begin with. You have to look at both the physiology and psychology behind behavior. In our case, these traits are deep rooted in our evolutionary journey. Back to a time when modern speech wasn't an available tool for us, a time when non-verbal gestures were the name of the game when it came to signaling our thoughts, feelings and emotions.

The question for us today is simply how much of this ancestral legacy do we still hold onto? The answer is certainly a substantial amount, and that is largely due to our limbic system or our "old mammalian brain".

Regardless of how much we have developed as individuals or civilization and society have in general, we still cannot fully escape the influence these primitive brain structures have over us. Analyzing people is really only about reading the signals these subconscious systems are setting off. As I have already mentioned, they stem from a time when non-verbal gestures and cues were the only mode of communication we had, and therefore are extremely difficult for us to mask.

However we do still learn a lot from our environment. Larger more conscious movements and mannerisms of the limbs can be culturally rooted. That is why it's important to assess the contextual cues first and foremost. This starts with assessing the cues which are likely to trigger off certain behavioral traits. These can be both external and internal, but will always be the subsequent driver of the proceeding behavior.

The next thing to watch out for is the changes, the sequences of signals which allow you to more easily pick up on mood. Large shifts in body language displays will almost always occur in clusters or in a grouping of mannerisms, allowing you to much more reliably pick up on these changes when they do occur. The fourth consideration is regarding the character and culture of the individual or group of people you are assessing. As I mention, the subconscious cues are almost always the same within everyone, but the larger and more overt body movements and gestures can be very much interpersonal, depending on somebody's upbringing and background. Try to assess for their baseline behavior and make adjustments to your thinking either way.

Only then can you start to move onto analyzing the specific parts of the body when reading a person, to truly assess the thinking behind their behavior. This starts with the lower limbs, the legs and feet. People often neglect to pick up on the signals from these body parts as they wrongly presume that they do not hold much weight. However this is untrue, as the signals given via the legs and feet give very significant signs. They are under much less conscious control and often go unnoticed. So can give very genuine signals as a result, so should not be dismissed. Subconscious crossing and/or pointing of the knees and legs will say a lot about a person's attentiveness and mood.

The same can be said of the arms and hands in terms of crossing and general direction. However due to the more intricate and expressive ways in which they can be controlled, the arms, and especially the hands can give an even greater range of non-verbal gestures. Make sure that you give special attention to the interaction the hands make with other body parts, such as those of the head and face. Gestures given as a standalone can be very powerful cues, however when they are performed in conjunction with others, that signal amplifies even more so. Most people typically only concentrate on facial features and head movements when it comes to analyzing others, and I can see why.

These signals are of high significance, even compared with the arms and hands. The facial features are almost always in sight and under the most conscious control compared with any other body part. Hence special effort is usually given in an attempt to not give anything away here, people even practice their "poker face" in the mirror. This brings us onto the specific deception detectors. The signals which potentially give away untruthful behavior. These "tells" regarding the face, only have to be minor. A flushing of the face or flicker of the eyebrow often enough to suggest a hidden agenda.

Also watch out for the interactions of the hands with the nose/ears and mouth. Touching of any one of these areas will signify something. It may just be a genuine momentary bout of nerves, or maybe something more sinister the person is attempting to mask. But as always, make sure you watch out for excess movement and fidgeting from any body part, be it the hands, feet or eye lids. If there is one "tell" which signifies general unease and possible deception most accurately, it is this.

Good Luck!

CPSIA information can be obtained
at www.ICGtesting.com
Printed in the USA
LVHW081934131120
671646LV00023B/421/J

9 781801 202800

IN THIS BOOKLET, WE WILL
TRAVEL TO THE OTHER WORLD,
THE WORLD OF MYTHS AND
LEGENDS IN MOROCCAN
FOLKLORE.

AISHA KANDISHAH ,
MULE GRAVES
HAMO ONAMIR
ISLE & TESLET

ALL OF WHICH WERE
ENTERTAINED BY STORIES
ABOUT MYTHS TRAVERSED IN
THE PAST, BUT THEIR IMPACT
CONTINUES TO THIS DAY.

Contents :

2

Moroccan culture is full of many

fairy tales that some believe may be true while they remain just myths that our grandfathers and grandmothers told us during childhood.

What distinguishes these fairy tales is their diversity, including scary horror stories about the supernatural

There are also romantic dramatic stories

These stories and myths have not only remained in the past, but that their impact continues to this day. Some of them have left a psychological impact on the imagination of many people thinking that they are true stories that actually occurred, as we said at the beginning,

And some of them left us with annual customs and traditions that are celebrated by some regions here in Morocco.

THE LEGEND

OF

AISHA KANDISHA

Aisha Kandisha is considered one of the most popular characters of the jinn

(Jinn are creatures that live in the same world but cannot be seen usually, and they are supernatural that our senses perceive, and have minds and understanding,)

in the Moroccan folklore. The folk song deals with it and describes it as "Aisha Moulat el-Marjeh" or "The Lady of the Swamps" as the song describes it. She is also described by various titles, including "Lalla Aisha", "Aisha Al-Sudania" or "Aisha. Gnaouia »according to the different regions of Morocco,

The legend talks about a beautiful woman named Aisha Qandisha who fascinates men with her beauty and lures them to her den where she has sex with them and then kills them and feeds on the flesh and blood of their bodies.

Therefore, everyone who is led by chance to the places in which it is located

She seduces him, and leads him behind her, unconscious to where she is hidden, without being able to resist,, and there she devours him mercilessly, after he sleeps with her to extinguish her constant hunger for flesh and human blood.

What distinguishes her from the rest of the women is her feet that resemble the legs of a camel, and the only way to escape from her is self-control and surprise her with fire because she is considered her weakness.

There are many realistic accounts of the famous biography of "Aisha Qandisha" in the Moroccan folklore,

There are those who indicated that she lived in the fifteenth century. She is a jihadist woman who lived in the fifteenth century. The Portuguese called her Aisha Kundisha (Countess: means princess), meaning Princess Aisha. And it cooperated with the Moroccan army then to fight the Portuguese.

Religion killed its people because of the skill and courage it showed in the fight, so that some, led by the Portuguese, thought that it was not a human but a genie, and this recognition has continued to prevail in Morocco to this day.

She is – in another novel – a Moroccan woman whose husband was killed by Portuguese colonialism between the fifteenth and eighteenth centuries, so she decided to take revenge on him and became fierce resistance to him. She was also a "countess", meaning an Andalusian princess, who was expelled from Andalusia. Colonist resistance.

The stories that circulate the biography of this strange and mysterious character are many, in which reality intersects with myth, and the superstitious aspect overcomes it so much that it is difficult to decide whether this character is real or just a myth of the Moroccan popular imagination. At times, she is a fairy with a beautiful female body and the feet of a camel or a mule. She takes the valleys, wells, and caves as her abode.

She charms men with her beauty and lures them to her den where she kills them and feeds on the flesh and blood of their bodies. She is only afraid of one thing, which is the fire in front of her. Some of them claimed that she blocked the path of men who were living in the villages and nearly beat them, but they managed to escape by burning their turbans in front of them. Fire is its weakness.

Moroccan folklore also depicts Qandisha in the form of an envious old witch, who spends all her time playing games to separate husbands, and again in the image of a beautiful woman with feet that resemble the hooves of goats, camels or mules. (According to Moroccan regions).

The biography of "Aisha Qandishah", despite her multiple novels, became the most famous story circulated for generations in Morocco, and the narrators acted in a manner that made her oscillate between reality and myth,

11

between positive and negative, and also became the subject of rich research for a large number of sociologists and anthropologists in the world such as the Finnish anthropologist and Stermark westermark (1862/1939) who compared this venerable side fairy with "Ishtar", the ancient goddess of love that was sacred to the peoples of the Mediterranean and Mesopotamia from the Carthaginians, Phoenicians, and Canaanites who used to perform sacred rituals in her honor. He assumed that Aisha Qandisha was the Queen of Heaven. When the ancient Semites believed that it inhabited eyes, rivers, seas, and wet areas in general. It was also covered by the Moroccan sociologist of French origin Paul Pascon (1958/1932) in his book "Myths and Beliefs from Morocco".

And the myth of Qandisha's life is similar to several eastern and strange myths for others, such as the Egyptian myth Al-Nadha, which is about a beautiful woman who appears in dark nights in the fields to call the name of a certain person, so this person gets bewitched and follows the call until he reaches her and then they find him dead the next day, and the western legend is the bloody Mary And she is a woman who comes out of the mirror when her name is mentioned three times in a dark room while standing in front of the mirror

She comes out with a knife and blood on her face and wears a white dress with her shaggy hair. The myth of "Aisha Qandisha" is also similar to the myth of the Gulf, "Umm Duwais", a myth about a beautiful fairy who pursues men at night and makes them fascinated by her beauty, as soon as they are astonished by her. She pursues her and does not stop until she kills and eats them.

THE LEGEND

OF

MULE GRAVES

The myth of the mule of the graves, or as some call it "the torment of the graves" or "Tamghart Nasmadal" in the Berber dialect, meaning the bride of the graves. An abbreviated mule comes out of the graves in the blackness of the darkness and continues to run in a crazy manner that does not stop until the beginning

of the morning, while in the darkness of the night it looks like a flying flame of fire. People refer to this to the tremendous sparks that emanate from her eyes, and it is said that she breaks the silence and calm of the night with the The noise it makes and brings by its hooves and twisting;

Of the huge iron chains fastened to her neck, which makes everyone in a state of great fear and terror .

The grave mule is a name given to a woman who lived in a long time ago, and her story goes back to that she was a wife who lived with her husband alone a decent and stable lifeThey do not lack anything from the pleasures of life while they live in it, until the husband died suddenly one day, and the widowed wife remained alone in deep grief, wearing a white dress, during the waiting period. In her home, the waiting period is called, and it is four months and ten days, and during this period, which is called the waiting period, the woman does not have to reveal herself to those who are forbidden to her according to Islamic law)

But that miserable widow committed a major sin, which is the crime of adultery during this waiting period,

And as the myth says, it is what she did, and the woman turned into half a mule and half a human, and her eyes became red, the fire caught fire, and her ends were tied to baskets running behind her, and she became stronger than before.

She sleeps with the dead during the day and then shakes at night, wandering around the graves and attacking men, Only his victims.

Men were killed or buried alive by her hands, and some accounts say that she is hiding in the form of an acquaintance of the village members Which she.

It is said that if this mule encounters any man during her wanderings at night, she carries him on her back to the cemetery in which she lives, and there she digs a large grave for him and either bury him alive or eats it and leaves nothing of it, and in the absolute she does not harm women at all.

And in some accounts about it, she enters the houses during the day, and if night falls, she kidnaps the man of the house and escapes with him to the cemetery to pay the price for that man who disobeyed God with him for a long time, and some say that she tormented her prey before eating or burying him, so she would cut off her genitals from men to avenge herself and all the women of Eve Of men.

It is narrated that an elderly woman, when he was in his youth in the fifties, was returning from the woods at night heading towards the headquarters of his tribe, then he passed by a dark cemetery unknown with his flashlight. Meanwhile, he heard the sounds of steps approaching him accompanied by the sounds of chains. At first the man thought that an animal was following his track, but soon he heard the sound of a loud cry as if it were a female suffering or that someone was tearing her alive. He kept running randomly until he reached a carob tree inside the forest and climbed over it, wishing himself to be saved, but the strange animal pursued him and kept trying to uproot the carob tree from its roots, and the man lies over it and sees only two eyes like a volcano, and only hears strange sounds that the animal makes from time to time.

The man remained above the tree until the call to prayer rose suddenly and the creature fled, and the man remained on the tree until the light of day brightened, and he was surprised that he was in the center of the cemetery exactly and did not realize that, so he went down to it and went to his tribe, and when he told them what happened to him they knew that what he attacked was the mule of the graves Which they heard its legend when they were young.

And in another narration that some women went out one day with their men and sons, traveling between the valleys, and the convoy settled in a place near a cemetery as far as the eye could see, and they all settled to rest from the trouble of traveling, to continue their early morning journey.

Women woke up in the morning to find that their men were nothing but the bones, just as one or more predators ate their bodies while they slept, except that it was the mule of the graves, as myths say. It is difficult to believe that there is a creature on the face of the earth that can devour a large number of men in one night.

THE MYTH

OF

HAMO ONAMIR

The legend of HAMO ONAMIR is not just a story that can be read by literary reading only, but it is greater than that, because it carries deep elements that must be subject to a deep anthropological reading, it is a myth in which metaphors are used to express the eternal spirit in Amazigh culture ...

The legend talks about an orphan named "Hamo Onamir" who was of dazzling beauty and lived with his mother who raised him well and brought him into the mosque to learn reading, writing and memorizing the Quran. Once in days and years, Onamir became a young man, even the most beautiful young man in the village, loved by all

And they admired his beauty, splendor and literature.

And they admired his beauty, splendor and literature.

One day he woke up early as usual to go to the mosque, but he was surprised by something strange, as he noticed that his hands were decorated with the henna

(Henna is extracted from the henna plant, and most people in the Arab countries, India and Pakistan use it to dye their hair. Henna is also used to make beautiful engravings on the hands and is used to treat many diseases.)

When he went to The mosque, al-Faqih

(A researcher interested in studying and teaching the Qur'an and Islamic jurisprudence)

scolded him and ordered to beat him so that he would not put henna in his hands again. On the next day, Onamir found his hands once again decorated with henna, and the al-Faqih struck him again, and this was repeated for several days until the al-Faqih realized that Onamir was wronged and said to him: "Don't sleep this night until you know who puts henna in your hands."

Onamir did what al-Faqih He recommended him, and he did not sleep that night and waited for a long time while pretending to sleep, until he saw a row of nymphs coming from the sky and surrounding him and began to put henna in his hands , Onamiller was so

27

impressed with their dazzling beauty,
they went out one by one and
disappeared into the dark before dawn.
In the morning Onamir told him
everything he had seen. Al-Faqih told
him: "This time, take a thread and a
needle with you, tie the mermaid's
clothes to your clothes, and when they
want to leave, release them one by one
until the turn of the last of them comes.

If she asks you to release her, tell her that
you want to marry her."

Unamir actually brought the thread and
the needle, and pretended to sleep. And
when the nymphs came he sewed their
clothes with his clothes. And when they
wanted to leave, they were not able to do

Then they began to shout: We ask you, Onamir, to set us free so that we can join our people in the sky before morning. onamir released them. one after another.

And when the last turn came, he told her that he wanted her to be his wife, and the mermaid answered him: "Let me go to my family, because you will not be able to fulfill my claim.

Onamir replied, "I will do what you instruct me and keep all my promises." She said, "I want a house with seven rooms that are locked with one key, and keep it a secret I keep it so no one will ever see me."

Onamir agreed and built her a seven-room house, one inside the other, and put her in the last room. And he used to lock the seven doors with one key, which he kept so that no one would see his secret.

One day, the mermaid asked Onamir to bring her venison and he took his horse, after he had hidden the key in a pile of haystacks. On that day, his mother heard a rooster shouting: "I have found the key of the Onamer with which he closes the seven rooms. She was so happy, she opened the doors of the rooms one by one, until she reached the last room, and found the mermaid sitting, combing her long black hair, and the place had lit up with her beauty. She started scolding her and insulting her and saying to her: "What are you doing here? Go where you came from!" Then the doors closed and returned the key to his place.

Onamir returned from the hunt and found the nymph weeping and the ground was wet with her tears. He asked her why she was crying and she said: You did not fulfill your promise to me and tell others your secret. Then she asked him to open the window to get some air. He suffered from her grief and opened the window for her, so she went out and headed towards the sky, saying:

Goodbye Onamir. If you want to see me again, follow me to sky. "

Days passed and he did not eat, drink or sleep. One day, he decided to find a way up to the sky.

So he took his horse and said goodbye to his mother, and set off traveling from country to country asking everyone he met on his way

One day while traveling, he met an old man, whom Onamir told of his story and told him he wanted to go to heaven. The old man looked at him for some time and said to him: "I have the solution to your problem, and the only way to reach the sky is for the great eagle in the green

mountain to carry you." He was so happy
when he heard the old man's words,
Onamir thanked him so much

And he set off towards the green
mountain, and it took him several years
until he reached him, so he called to the
great eagle and told him his story, then
the eagle told him: Your story is very sad,
but I have become an old eagle, tired and
my feather has begun to fall. If you want
me to carry you to the sky, then slay your
horse and feed me From his flesh until
his wings regain their ability to fly!
Onamir could not slaughter his friend,
the horse that accompanied him on his
long journey, so the horse said to him:

If I am to put an end to your torture, kill me. So you can reach your wife in the sky Onamer slaughtered his horse while he was weeping and fed the eagle from him until his strength returned to him and sprouted his feathers, and he saved seven pieces of meat to feed him during the trip. The eagle carried Unamir on his back and told him not to speak,

He took him towards the sky and was feeding him from the Seven Pieces each time the powers of the old eagle would decrease until they came close to reaching However, the eagle felt tired again and its strength began to diminish. Onamir took the last piece of meat to feed it to him, but it fell from him unintentionally. He found no solution except to cut off a part of his body and feed it to the eagle so that it could continue flying That is what Onamir did amputate his hand and gave it to him Until his power returned to him.

Finally, the eagle drove him to the sky. Onamir sat at a spring of water, looking at the trees with wonderful leaves and wonderful fruits, until he saw a nymph in a running river and said to her: "I beg you to show me the whereabouts of a nymph. I am Onamir coming from the earth. The nymph knew him well.

She was also visiting him on those nights

I took him to the place he wanted, and there he found his wife feeling very happy, and he forgot all the torment that he had gone through on earth. The nymph Onamir showed everything in her palace until she reached a stone placed in a small hole and said to him: "Never move this stone."

Days passed. Unamir felt nostalgic for his mother and was impatient to leave her, so he lifted the stone Forgetting the advice of the mermaid he looked out from the hole on the ground and saw his mother alone. And she got blind

From the great crying of her son while she was holding a sheep and she said: If my son Onamir was present, he would have slaughtered the sacrifice of the Eid with his hand.."

Onamir shouted: "I am here, mom. I am coming to you. I will never make you sad again!"

He threw himself from the hole to the ground, and the wind began to tear him until drops of blood fell on the ground, some drops fell on the neck of the sheep and slaughtered it, and others fell on his mother's eyes, so her eyesight returned to her……..

Our hero couldn't live apart from his mother or his wife, so he decided

Sacrifice his body and let his soul live with them.

The legend of Onamir is replete with symbols that must be deciphered. His ascent to the sky, how do we understand it, as well as his relationship with the nymphs and the fact that they exist or not ...

Despite the presence of a whiff of Islamic culture through the image of the imam of the mosque, it is likely that this myth is older than Islam itself, and that the other secrets it contains extends deep into Amazigh history, and it remains just a myth that is difficult to believe.

ASLI & TESLET

LEGEND

According to the Moroccan Berbers, the story is a myth of love that crosses the ages, known as Asli and Teslit, and in the Berber language it means (bride and groom). This name is known for two lakes in one of the Michelin regions.

is located in the heart of the High Atlas Mountains in southeastern Morocco,

at an altitude of 2,220 meters..

inhabited by the Ait Hadidou Berber They are tribes that depend on work in the fields of agriculture and livestock tribes who settled there, according to historians in the 17th century,

Teslit or Taslit or Taljunga is a character from the Amazigh culture, and Tesselet or Taslit is an Amazigh word that means fiancée or bride

Teslit is the sweetheart of her lover Asli, who is also, a character from the Amazigh culture, and it is an Amazigh word meaning a preacher or groom.

They sincerely loved each other,

They were promised that they would not be allowed Nothing whatsoever by separating them But Asli was from a tribe hostile to the tribe he loved, and this was the obstacle that stood between the two lovers.

Our story happened Amidst these thorns of hatred, where the rose of love grew between Moha and Hada

Young Moha, a scion of the Ait Ibrahim tribe, fell in love with a girl named Hadda from the Ait Azza tribe. The two lovers met in secret again and again from the people of their villages, under the shade of the trees scattered in the woods. But one day, Moha and Hadda decided to get married and put an end to all of this so that they could live under one roof. However, as expected, the two tribes together rejected this marriage and prevented the two lovers from meeting each other, so that they would break the pillars of the love between them.

Haddah decided to lock herself in her room without eating or drinking, grieving over the forced separation of her lover, as Moha did the same. And when it seemed to them that marriage was some impossible They could not bear preventing their innocent relationship from all the disputes that existed between the two tribes and which they had no part in. The two lovers seemed to cry and shed many tears, and thanks to that, two lakes were formed. ..

The first came feminine according to its name among the people of the region who spoke Amazigh, "Tesleet", and she is

43

the bride who is located near the Ait Yazza tribe. The vicinity of the village of Emlschel (about 6 km);

The second lake is "Asal", which is the groom, which is located in the geographical area of the Ait Ibrahim tribes.

Another story says that both lovers left his tribe towards the mountains. The young man drowned himself in a lake now called Lake Asli, while the girl drowned herself in a lake called "Taslit"... But whatever the stories differ, the meaning remains that the two sailors are closely linked to a forbidden love story whose ending was tragic..

Years passed, until the hostility between the Ait Ibrahim tribe and the Ait Azza tribe disappeared, and the people of the region did not forget that old sunken love And to atone for their sin, he decided to call the two lakes "Isli and Teslit" (the bride and groom) to fulfill an inspiring and intense dream of marriage - symbolically - even after their. drowning. And even more than that; The two tribes decided to have a permanent son-in-law relationship .. Until it became an annual anniversary in what is now called in Morocco. the engagement season, where the marriage season is between loversEngagement season in Amelichel is held annually in September,

Young men from the region choose their brides before the season starts.

And during it, honorable popular celebrations are held within the framework of a group wedding after the marriage of a large number of husbands.

And this season is crowded with people, as it is attended by many visitors from different cities of Morocco, as well as foreign tourists.

And it remains the only thing that exists now As for the myth, there is no evidence to prove its authenticity, and what is closest to the truth is that it is nothing but a myth.

How long did we wait for the night in our childhood years to be able to hear Stories of jinn , fairies , Monsters, princesses and other fictional charactersfrom our great-grandfathers and grandmothers. We were just wrapping around them and enjoying the way they tell them and how they tell these stories until we really, at that time, thought they were real stories and they actually happened. However, most of it was a figment of their imagination, and the other was a myth of history.

Printed in Great Britain
by Amazon

33747991R00030